MW01611857

e2

effectiveelders

FOREWORD

When the time was exactly right, Christ launched His church to be the body *through which* He has continued *the work He had begun in* His body as Jesus of Nazareth. As that church authentically followed His design, it was right for the time; and the time was right for that church.. This convergence produced a movement so magnificent that we might find it hard to believe what happened in the next few decades it if it were not a matter of history.

Today, we are facing a convergence very much like that one twenty centuries ago. On one hand, this is a time of crisis. The world as we have known it—politically, economically, socially, culturally, and personally—is being shaken to its roots and threatens to collapse. People are becoming desperate for solutions but none is appearing on the horizons of human efforts and resources.

On the other hand, a transformation is emerging among churches as they become determined to be what Jesus intended His church to be and to do.

As these two factors converge, authentic Christianity is an idea whose time has come; and, as Victor Hugo said, there is nothing more powerful than that. It is stronger, he said, than all the armies of the world. An invasion of armies can be resisted, but not an idea whose time has come.

For half a century the name of Peter Drucker has been a byword in the business world. Late in life, he turned his attention to supporting this movement to restore the original character and character of churches. This, he said, is the most important social phenomenon of our day. The future of America, he said, is in the hands of the churches—not in the hands of government, politics, human agencies, or corporations. As these churches become more and more like the Biblical church than the model than has become so

3

common among churches, they become amazingly effective. Yes, a thrilling awakening is stirring among churches!

The authenticity and effectiveness of a local church is in direct proportion to the spiritual maturity, skills and commitment of its leaders, especially its elders. Therefore, selecting, training, supporting, challenging, and equipping elders in every way must be a highest priority in every congregation.

The function of leadership in most churches today has been impaired by an unintentional importing of assumptions and habits from: our histories, the cultures around us, the secular business world, and the world of politics. But in the awakening churches, a model of leadership that harkens back to the church of the New Testament is arising.

Leadership development is more than a process of transferring information, as imperative as that is. This must be supported by processes and experiences that transform the ideas into action. This encompasses practice in team-building, active processing and application of ideas, social-emotional support, sustenance for leaders' families, resource sharing, and even cultivating physical health. This dimension of growth is supported as leaders participate in events such as seminars; retreats; and time spent together in Bible study, fellowship, and prayer.

I appreciate the role of elders in the local church and I long to see the "clergy-laity" dichotomy healed. I have had experience both as preacher and elder; and I am committed to helping these roles become a synergistic partnership in the Body of Christ.

I want to commend Jim, Dave and Gary and the good work they have done through these four volumes. Every elder in the church should purchase and read these works. As the leadership of any church goes, so goes the church. Elders who use these volumes will be better prepared to lead the body of Christ. I highly recommend these works and pray that the Lord will use them to strengthen and equip men to effective do the work that God has called them to do.

Joe Scott Ellis PhD (1928-2013)
Cincinnati, Ohio

Note: Dr. Joe Ellis was our instructor, colleague, friend, an inspiration to all those who knew him, and a Kingdom-minded servant leader.

Enjoy
Table of Contents

Introduction

Introduction to *Enjoy*

I wish you could be here. We are sitting around a table at Skyline Chili in Cincinnati, Ohio . . . a familiar venue for anyone who attended Cincinnati Christian University. What started over a picnic table with coffee in Heiligenkreuz, Austria now reaches its conclusion over a plate of chili in Cincinnati, Ohio. When we met, we knew each other as mere acquaintances, but over the two years of sharing, thinking, planning, dining, and writing together . . . we have become friends. What  started as a working acquaintanceship has developed into an enjoyable friendship and partnership in ministry. When we first met, it was all work and no play, now it's work and play . . . with productivity. Scripture says, "Though one may be overpowered, two can defend themselves. A cord of three strands is not quickly broken" (Eccl. 4:12). Relationships are not only a natural part of life, but a necessity for serving in a congregation. Learning to live in community, enjoying the relationships into which God has called us, enables us to serve as elders and leaders within the congregation.

It is amazing the strides we will take to maintain relationships, i.e. Facebook, MySpace, Twitter, email and texting, not to mention the commonality of cell phones. We gather at reunions with family, classmates, and friends from the military or business. We meet for coffee in a local establishment, or even take time to send an old fashioned letter. We value relationships because we value the people in them, and we recognize that relationships do not maintain themselves.

One may not think of relationships as a matter of stewardship. However, once you recognize that the relationships in our lives are given by God and have impacted who you are, we must give them proper attention so as to reflect Christ in them, so as to let them serve as an example to others. We must recognize relationships as part of God's design for the church and its leadership. Without recognizing this, we fail to be proper stewards of those God has brought into our lives, those whom we serve and with whom we serve.

As an elder, one has to acknowledge that leadership requires relationships. Elders were meant to serve as a team, not solo. No leader is an island unto himself, unless he is leading a church of one. Consider the opposite: What would an elder who is *not* a steward of relationships be like? Disengaged, conspicuously absent from church events, family that seems more dysfunctional than functional, cliquish and closed to new people. Elders must exemplify Christ in their relationships with others. For example, Scripture is quite clear in its expectations that an elder must exemplifying family life and being a good steward of family relationships, begging the question, how can I be a better steward of my family relationships..

In *Answer* (first volume in this series), four essential elder relationships were mentioned about the qualifications for service: God, self, family, and others. While this chapter is not intended to be treatise on relationships, it would be remiss not to at least highlight some basic relational principles for exemplary relationships. Each of these four principles can be applied to the four essential relationships for an elder. The four relationship principles are Cultivate, Communicate, Confess, and Celebrate. If we are to be stewards of our relationships, we must apply these four principles whenever possible.

Cultivating relationships means that you want to establish new relationships. Elders should endeavor to make new relationships, to expand their range of influence through intentionally building relationships with others. For example, how might we cultivate relationships with others? Elders may have to intentionally be visible, engaging of new members and guests, and even actively participate in routine church activities and special events.

Being a steward of relationships likewise requires us to *communicate* with one another. Consider this: How many relationship issues could be avoided with clearer communication? How many issues do elders handle that deal with better communication? For example, how can we be better stewards of our family relationships? Perhaps having a family meeting wherein family members can share with each other ideas, concerns, calendar items, or even special requests. If you don't provide attention to communication, it may not happen on its own.

Realizing it is a long-standing cliché, "Love means never having to say you're sorry" is still used today . . . it's just *not* true. Individuals who are unwilling to acknowledge shortcomings, ask for forgiveness, and recognize their own faults rarely find themselves in healthy relationships. *Confession* is a vital part of maintaining sound Christian relationships. Confession to God, confession to family, one another, and even to one's self is vital to healthy and sustained relationship. It is a reminder that perfectionism has no room in Christian relationships.

Finally, relationships need to *celebrate*! We celebrate the events that define our relationships and us. We celebrate weddings and anniversaries, birthdays and funerals, and significant family events, like adoptions, baptisms, graduations, or retirements. We celebrate not only to remember the event, but also to maintain our relationships. We schedule celebrations to give a pretext to getting together and sharing with one another. In short, we are stewards of our relationships through our celebrations with one another.

Healthy congregations require a healthy leadership. Without a healthy leadership, the odds of a congregation growing spiritually, let alone numerically, are greatly diminished. This is the principle concern of this series: Healthy leadership facilitates healthy congregational life. To ensure healthy congregations, we must give attention to the health of our leadership, the elders. This book endeavors to orient, inform, challenge, educate, and ultimately equip men to be leaders within the congregation, elders that genuinely lead and shepherd the flock of God. It calls us to reflect in our character the character of Christ while serving as elders within His body.

Leadership that is Christian is based on God's *call* to service, one to which we must *Answer*. The man is qualified and equipped by a life representative of Christian *character*, maturity, we *Reflect His character*. Further, an elder must possess *competencies*, abilities that serve him well as he leads and shepherds God's people; *Lead* His congregation. Finally, the *community*, both the congregation and its social context, provide the area for an elder to serve as a leader within the community of faith and a witness to the community around it as we *Enjoy* His people. All four are essential for Christian leadership to be effective, none of them are optional. *Enjoy*, Volume 4, addresses the relationships of an elder as a leader in the congregation and community.

About the Series

This book is the second of a four volume designed to equip elders for effective leadership in the congregation by e2 ministries (www.e2elders.org). The four volumes (*Answer, Reflect, Lead, and Enjoy*) parallel the four basic components of Christian leadership previously explained. These books are not intended to be scholarly treatises of the eldership. Rather, they are designed as useful study guides that utilize practical and academic insights for elders. Each chapter is intentionally brief and concludes with reflective questions for your own personal use, or use as an eldership as a means of training and equipping one another for service.

Reflect, Volume 2, addresses the character of an elder as a leader in the congregation and community. Chapter 1 asserts the necessity of a Christian mind among the eldership; one that has been transformed by Christ and no longer conforms to the world's pattern. Chapter 2 addresses the spiritual lives of elders, asking them to reflect a growing relationship with God; with Chapter 3 addressing one key element of spiritual life, prayer. Chapter 4 is on protecting one's character, with recommendations on how to avoid burnout or spiritual and moral failure; while Chapter 5 addresses restoring one's character and the character of others, with an emphasis on confidentiality among the eldership. The final chapter discusses the value and importance of having elders accountable to other elders, spiritually and pastorally.

This book can be used in two ways. First, it can be used as an individual study, something that you as an individual elder within the congregation read for your own edification and education. You may be a new elder, or perhaps an experienced leader looking for additional perspective and insight. Regardless, this book integrates throughout the text a set of Reflection Questions designed to help you apply each chapter to your life as a Christian and an elder. A second way in which this book can be used is by your eldership. Each elder could read the book, use the Reflection Questions, but then make use of them to discuss the text together as an eldership. In either case, whether individual or group, we do hope the book is beneficial to your life and ministry.

About the Authors

This series is not the product of one author. Rather, it is the fruit of three individuals' labor, working in concert with one another, and bringing their diverse experience and perspective to the table for discussion. One of the authors is a churchman, Gary Johnson, another is a church consultant, David Roadcup, and still another is an academic, James Estep. While these three men have known one another separately for a long time, it was not until they were all three together in Heiligenkreuz, Austria teaching students from eastern Europe and central Asia at *Haus Edelweiss* (TCMI) that the three men sat together for the first time and shared their concerns for the health of congregations and the health of its leadership. We are convinced that a healthy leadership builds a healthy congregation. From these initial conversations over coffee a hemisphere away came the idea for this series, designed to strengthen the health of elders as the congregation's leaders.

While individuals were assigned their own chapters to write, the final form of each chapter was reviewed and reworked by all three authors sharing a common table. Hence, the work is a tri-authored resource for the equipping of congregational leaders who serve as elders of the Church. It further led to the founding of e2: effective elders ministries in June 2012 (www.e2elders.org).

We are praying for you and your congregation, and if we may be of service, feel free to contact us at your convenience.

July 2013

James Estep, Jr., Ph.D.
Dean, School of Undergraduate Studies
Lincoln Christian University
Lincoln, Illinois
Jim@e2elders.org

David Roadcup, D.Min.
Professor of Christian Ministries
Cincinnati Christian University
Cincinnati, Ohio
David@e2elders.org

Gary Johnson, D.Min.
Senior Minister
Indian Creek Christian Church
Indianapolis, Indiana
Gary@e2elders.org

Chapter 1

Enjoying Your Family

James Riley Estep, Jr.

Comedian George Burns once said, "Happiness is having a large, loving, caring, close-knit family in another city." We are all part of a family. Regardless of the structure of our family or the dynamics within it, we live in the community of the family. We were born into one, grew up in one, and started a new one. We identify ourselves in term of family: son, brother, husband, father, etc. While God identifies His people with many metaphors, He does use the imagery of the family to describe the church.

- "Therefore, as we have opportunity, let us do good to all people, especially to those who belong to the *family of believers*" (Gal. 6:10).
- "For this reason I kneel before the Father, from whom *his whole family* in heaven and on earth derives its name" (Eph. 3:14-15).
- "Both the one who makes men holy and those who are made holy are of the *same family*. So Jesus is not ashamed to call them brothers" (Heb. 2:11-12).

How does the notion of family, elders and the church all fit together? We really cannot separate our life in the family with our life as leaders in the church. Perhaps the insights of a 9-year old girl demonstrate the point. I was teaching an adult Sunday school class teaching when the question came up, "Why are all the elder's men? Why are they not women?" Not wanting to quickly retort with the appropriate "Book, Scripture, and verse," I wanted to explain why Scripture would indicate a male leadership within the church, and be sensitive *not* to unduly start a controversy. One of the couples in the class let their daughter sit in with them that day, and she jumped up and exclaimed, "Elders are the daddies of the church!" I had never really thought of such a simple statement.

God wants us to enjoy our families. We draw strength from them, insights on life from them, and serve together with them. An elder does not stand alone as a leader in the church, but as a leader within his family and now in the family of God.

☺**Reflection Question:** In what ways is being a father similar to being an elder? How does your experience as a father aid in your ability to serve as an elder?

Challenges to an Elder's Family

All families, even Christian ones, face challenges. Christian families, endeavoring to set an example and live beyond the expectations of the world, perhaps find it even more challenging, and perhaps even more so for an elder's family. Without over simplifying the requirement, the elder is to be the husband/father of a healthy Christian family. "An elder must be blameless, the husband of but one wife, a man whose children believe and are not open to the charge of being wild and disobedient" (Titus 1:6). More explicitly, Paul explains, "He must manage his own family well and see that his children obey him with proper respect. (If anyone does not know how to manage his own family, how can he take care of God's church?)" (1 Tim. 3:4-5). It is no surprise that even in the first-century, a concern for the health of the family of church leaders is openly expressed. An elder's family faces all the typical stresses, strains, and foibles of any Christian home; but there may well be some additional challenges due to the role the husband/father has in the congregation.

First, Satan loves a fallen leader. An elder's ability to lead a congregation is reflected in his ability to lead his family. As explained above, his ability to manage his family demonstrates the qualities necessary as a leader of the church. When a leader's family becomes highly dysfunctional, it interrupts an elder's ability to concentrate on his work in the church, and detracts from his witness.[1] The families of elders are a prime target for the one who benefits most from their demise, Satan. For this reason, elders must first minister to their family, then to the congregation. Do not forget, your first responsibility is to your family relationships, then to the congregation.

Second, elders are in fact held to a higher standard. It is one thing for you to accept the call to serve as an elder; but with the acceptance of that call your family is also brought into the spotlight of the congregation and community. If families are not ready for this, or were perhaps not consulted before you made the decision, they may feel unfairly drawn into the public view of others. Consulting with your family about your call to serve and ministry as an elder, or asking them about it periodically afterward, would probably be advisable.

Third, elders have to confidentially deal with the dirt of the church. Anyone who has served as an elder for long realizes that they quickly become aware of issues involving other individuals and families in the church, financial concerns, troubles within the pastoral staff, troublesome members stirring up trouble, and immorality present in the congregation and community . . . and *cannot* share it with his family. We cannot simply deal with issues by sweeping the dirt under the proverbial rug, leaving a mound to trip on; but we have to address them confidentially, without public display. One of the strains of serving as an elder is being in relationship with a wife and children, and not being able to share everything you do. Even if you wanted to vent after a meeting, we cannot. Families face the challenge of being kept out of the loop while one member, you, are part of the loop.

Fourth, elders assume responsibility for the congregation's condition. Unlike those who simply "attend" church (more like worship), and simply partake of the fellowship of the congregation; elders are responsible for the administration of the congregation, its leadership and management. For this reason, elders and their families often face not only the typical stresses of how work or community impacts the family, but church plays a more significant place in their life. Elders face one more set of responsibilities, those posed by the congregation, this means some family resources (time, money, etc.) are expended by you in service of the church.

Fifth, elders face the criticism of others in the church. Unlike those who can simply slip in and slip out of worship, or go through the congregation "unnoticed" by others as innocent bystanders of the congregation's work; an elder certainly cannot do this. Elders face the criticism for decisions made and directions posed. While not all criticism is fair or accurate, elders are never going to please everyone. In fact, many times the criticism is based on incomplete information and the elder is not in a position to reveal the confidential information to adequately respond. The family of the elder is often harmed by collateral damage from any criticism or conflict with an elder. For this reason, as discussed in the previous book *Lead: His Church*, decision making must be done in a more objective and clearly articulated manner; and in this book the decision must be that of the elder and distanced from the members of your family. Before I can be an effective elder, I have to first be an effective husband and father.

☺**Reflection Question:** Which of these have you personally encountered? Can you think of personal illustrations, or situations of which you are aware, that would illustrate any of these.

The Dynamics of Family Relationships

While everyone wants to have a "healthy" family, often times we do not know the indicators of it nor do we know the warning signs of dysfunctional families. As elders, we have to enjoy our family, which means we have to try to have a healthy relationship within the family. Donald Joy, a family life ministry authority, has suggested that families exist in four different dynamic situations which he calls "family systems" (Figure 1.1).[2] Each system represents a unique relational dynamic that governs the family.

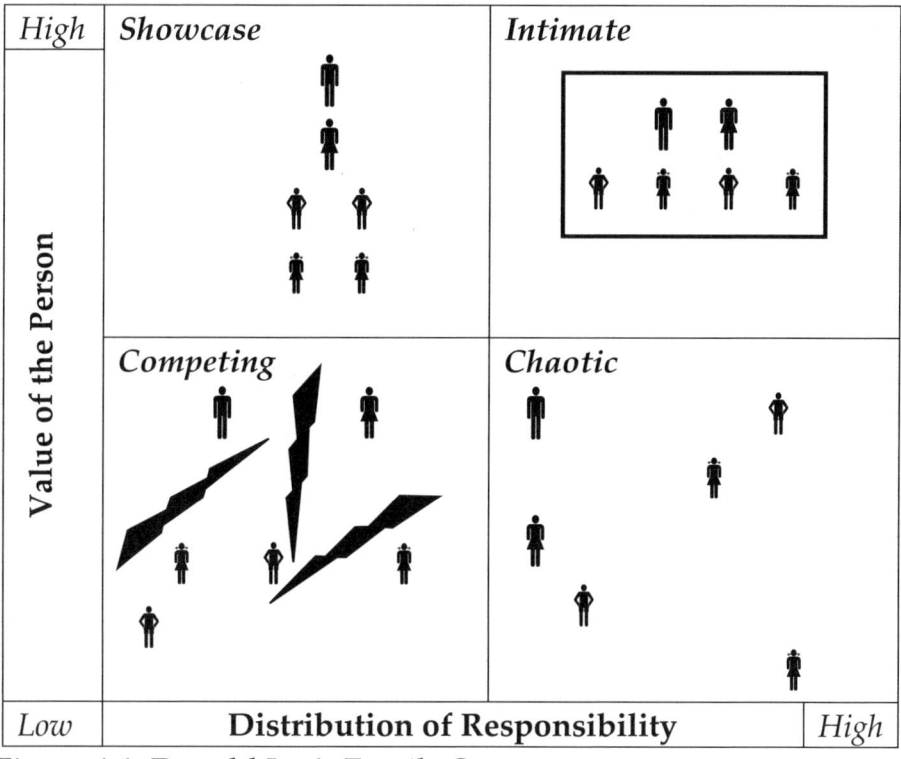

Figure 1.1: Donald Joy's Family Systems

The first is called *Showcase*. In this dynamic, the family's relationship is dominated by a hierarchical model of authority, favoring the male members. Like a chain-of-command, father to mother to oldest son, to next oldest son, to oldest daughter, and so on. The Showcase family emphasizes their public image to the extent that cover-ups are common and fault is often attributed to non-family members. For example, a son gets drunk, wrecks the car, injuring another driver; when the parents arrive, they get between the police and their son and excuse his behavior before even hearing the facts; and continue to do so even after learning of his intoxication and that the accident occurred in the on-coming lane. In such families, the "tournament male" is common, meaning the innate superiority of the male members of the family makes them feel invincible and infallible, leading to a high frequency of adultery in such families.

The *Competing* family dynamic places low value on family members and distribution of responsibilities within the family. It is characterized by conflict and division within the family. Because family members relate to one another in a spirit of competition, compulsive behaviors develop. We have all perhaps seen a family wherein "sibling rivalry" is present, but what if this rivalry extended to every member of the family? Each member of the family has a sense of superiority over the other, with a few members of the family taking responsibility for maintaining the fragmented family relationships. This dynamic is characterized by a family that seems to have an angry disposition, seeming to function within a continual state of conflict.

The third type of family dynamic is described as *Chaotic.* In these families the general rule is "everyone for themselves"! This is not the occasional load of undone laundry or the sporadic scheduling glitch; but a family relationship dominated by confusion and disorder. Little value is placed on members of the family, and no one really assumes responsibility for the family, without any order or structure to the family unit. Hence members use one another to fulfill their needs with casual disregard for the impact on other family members. Due to the low value of persons and the focus on immediate need gratification through means other than the family relationship, these families are characterized by a pronounced risk of drug or alcohol addiction in order to deal of the pressures of a chaotic lifestyle, as well as increased likelihood of sexual promiscuity in a search to find the intimacy missing in the family.

Naturally, the fourth option given by Joy is the *Intimate* family dynamic. As most may expect, it is characterized by a high value of family members, with each of its members assuming responsibility for the health of the family. In the intimate family there are definite roles, but without command structures, and there are also boundaries to the family, knowing who belongs, and structures based on relationship. While this may sound ideal . . . it is. The simple fact is that while the intimate family is ideal, no family is wholly in the upper right block on the chart. Elements of the other quadrants exist within every family. What is critical is that the primary dynamic reflects the Intimate family, with occasional incursions from the Showcase, Competing, and/or Chaotic family. Intimate families don't just happen by accident (if anything, the chaotic family is the one that simply happens), but rather needs to be nurtured and fostered by establishing relationships between each member of the family.

☺**Reflection Question:** Given the four basic family types, rank in order which dynamic seems to govern your family. What can you do to foster a more intimate family dynamic?

Rank	Family Dynamic and Comments
①	
②	
③	
④	

The Transitions of Family Relationships

We are not in this all alone. Families, by their nature, are communal . . . they require more than one individual, and are typically intergenerational, and that means each member of the family contributes to the dynamics of the unit. Likewise, families face predictable transitions, but are often ill prepared to anticipate or move through the various turns and bumps in family life.

Jack and Judith Balswick's discuss this in terms of parenting in their book *The Family: A Christian Perspective on the Contemporary Home*.[3] By discussing the transitions that children make upon a family, the Balswicks actually note the change in relationship between not only parent and child, but even between husband and wife, who are now perceived as dad and mom!

A Christian model of parenting leads to empowerment for maturity. The idea is that families are in a state of flux because they are designed not only to bring the next generation into existence, but launch them into independent adulthood as the child moves toward maturity. This process requires the family dynamic to transition through the process of moving from a newly-wed couple to an empty nest, a long-wedded couple? With the arrival of children, major changes occur in the family relationships. I can even remember never thinking of calling my wife "Mom," but on occasion that occurs now with children in the house. This signals more than a change in nomenclature, but a shift in thinking about our roles and relationships within the family. My wife was no longer my wife, but also mother to our children. The Balswicks suggest that parenting occurs along two general axes:

- "Parental Socioemotional Support" – relational interaction with the child through discussion and dialog
- "Parental Control" – providing direction to the child, one-way communication, providing for the child unilaterally

In infancy, the support dimension is low and the control is high. The child is dependent on the parents for everything, and parents are the providers. You may talk to the child, but it is not a conversation, its all one-way. Later, in early childhood and perhaps elementary age, the child is maturing, less dependent on the parents, for example, they can clothe, bathe, and feed themselves (the bottles and diapers are gone). This calls for a change in parenting strategies. Parents increase the support behaviors, teaching the child as the control aspect of their relationship begin to back off (since the child is no longer dependent upon the parent for everything). As the child enters adolescence another shift occurs. While teens may desire independence, they are really not ready for it; but they need to feel as if they are being treated differently  than before, during their even younger years. Once again, parenting shifts toward a more participatory model of relationship within the family, with a continued high level of support, such as not only discussing life with the teen but including them in on family planning. For example, it was probably safe during childhood to plan a family vacation unilaterally, but teens have school activities (even in the summer), jobs, and other commitments that feel trampled when parents don't at least give them a heads upon family plans. Teens are moving toward greater maturity, and hence the control dimension of the relationship diminished as the supportive nature of the relationship increases its two-way communication, bringing the teen into a quasi-adult status around the family table. Finally, the child enters adulthood. Young adults still need their parents, but not as before, and once again the dynamics of the family shift. "Launching" a child off on their own is a major transition. It calls for "low" levels of control and support, since they are probably no longer living in the family home, but in a dorm, apartment, or barracks.

Once again, the family goes through numerous transitions, each one changing the family dynamic and relationships within the family. Allow me to illustrate. Do you remember what it was like to be a married couple, the changes that occurred with the birth or adoption of your first child? Remember the first time you were able to leave your child/children with a sitter? How about the changes that a child entering school, and now having a new social network (especially new words) which not only called on a shift in parenting strategies, but how you relate to your wife? The child grows increasingly independent, and hopefully a matching level of maturity; do you know or remember what it was like to raise a teenager? (We had three in the house at once!) Remember the emotion of seeing your first child launch into adulthood? Also, what changes that brought to your family dynamic. I remember calling my parents when I went off to the university, and no one answered. I called, and called again, no answer. Something must be wrong. Finally, around 10:00pm, my parents answered. Now, I sounded like the parent, "Where have you been?!?" "We went out for dinner and a movie." "You never did that before!" "Well, we do now!" A family is a dynamic relational context that we all comprise and toward which we all contribute, there are no neutral bystanders. Changes to our families calls us to enjoy them in entirely new ways. First as couples, then as parents, children as infants and then the pride of seeing them grow and enter adulthood for themselves, and once again as couples enjoying the "empty nest" of senior life.

☺**Reflection Question:** Which phase of family life are you in currently? What challenges does it pose for you as both a father and elder?

Being a Family in the Family of God

With the challenges faced by elder's family, and dealing with the types of family systems that dominate the American home as well as the inevitable transitions within the family; *how does an elder balance his service to God's Kingdom and still serve his family?*

Elders have to remember that their primary responsibility is to their family, not the congregation. The congregation will survive without them, others can rise to the occasion to serve as a spiritual leader, but a husband and father are irreplaceable, and no one can simply step into that role in your absence. Remember, *prerequisite* to serving is having a healthy family, don't let serving disqualify you by harming your family.

An elder has to not only build a relationship with his wife, but must also guard her spiritual life and social integrity. While he may be closer to his wife than anyone else, sharing his life and love with her, she cannot always share with her his work as an elder. His wife should be his wife, not his peer-elder. People need to know that he is able to keep a confidence, and can segregate his familial relationships from his service in the church. I know of elders who come home after a meeting and use their wives as garbage disposals, dumping all the refuse upon them, venting frustration to them, and once he feels better, the wife is left to clean up the mess. As an elder, you have to first be your wife's husband, but also preserve her spiritual and social integrity by not making her a *defacto-elder*. Congregation members need to know that she doesn't know everything you do as an elder, and that they can relate to her as an individual, not simply the elder's wife. While there will be occasions where it is appropriate to share with your wife, please remember that you made the commitment to serve as elder, not her, and that too much sharing may confuse the role and relationship. Sharing more than the negatives and problematic situations of the church, but the advances and triumphs as well is critical for an elder's relationship with his wife.

Similar comments can be made about an elder's relationship with his children. Elders cannot simply pretend that serving as an elder doesn't impact his children and their relationship to others in the church. While this is true for all an elder's children, it is particularly of interest for an elder and his son(s), which is further discussed in Chapter 5. An elder must be careful what he shares about the congregation in front of his children. If he openly vents frustration or continuous critique of the congregation, its pastoral staff, or individual members of the congregation; this can have an adverse effect on his children's faith development, relationship with the congregation, as well as building barriers for their eventual service in the church. Share the positive images, successes, and the advancements of the church with children, building a favorable disposition toward it and serving within it.

☺**Reflection Question:** What challenges have you experienced in balancing your service as an elder and your family life? What challenges face your role as husband? What about as father?

If an elder's family is to model the Christian family, that not only includes the ideal image and expectations, but also how they deal with failure, immaturity, and relational strain. In this way, the elder's family *genuinely* reflects God's family, the church, when it not only models righteousness, but also forgiveness and care of souls.

Endnotes

---

[1] All families are to an extent "dysfunctional" because there are not perfect families. But, a genuinely dysfunctional family often doesn't recognize its dysfunction, regarding it to be "normal".

[2] The chart is an adaptation of Donald Joy's family systems found in *Risk Proofing Your Family* and is available from him for just $13. Just

send your request and return address along with a check or money order to Donald Joy, 1-5 Academy Drive, Wilmore, Kentucky 40390.

[3] Jack O. Balswick and Judity K. Balswick, *The Family: A Christian Perspective on the Contemporary Home* (Grand Rapids: Baker Book House, 2007), 117-119.

Chapter 2

Enjoying Your Father[1]

James Riley Estep, Jr.

"Jim, your dad's in the emergency room. It's not serious, but I'll call you if his condition changes." It was a call I had been regretting, but that I had received many times before. After hanging up the phone thoughts began to swell in my mind. What will it be like to lose my father? What lifelong impact has he made on my life? How is his life reflected in my own life? How are our lives different from one another? What will be his living legacy in my life? Hours passed as I pondered these thoughts, waiting for the inevitable ring of the phone. My father recovered, was released from the ER, and went home that same night. However, eleven months later, in the early hours of the morning, he passed away at home in his sleep with me by his side. I spoke at his funeral and shared family stories that shaped his life and mine.

I was left with the undeniable conclusion that my father has left an indelible impact on my life. For good or for ill, none of us are totally separate from our fathers. We have all been sons, and we are most probably all fathers. As an elder, we must be aware of all our relationships, and how they influence us as leaders, but the one that is perhaps overlooked is the impact made upon us by our fathers. We are sons, fathers, maybe grandfathers, and perhaps even great-grandfathers or even step fathers, it is one of our primary roles both in the family as well as in the congregation. We must enjoy our father's legacy in our lives by drawing from its advantages, and learning from its failings

Fathers and sons share an unparalleled relationship, one that continues to influence and impact us throughout our lives and even when our fathers have passed away. Yet, images of this relationship are often shaped by the stereotypes of Archie Bunker and "Meathead", Homer Simpson and Bart, Hank Hill and Bobby, and Peter Griffin's relationship with Chris and Stewie rather than the lens of Scripture. Discerning our relationship with our father has become an increasingly difficult task, regardless of what that relationship may be, it is one that must be reckoned with. This chapter will not simply explore the biblical portrayal of "father," but explain how the relationship with our fathers may influence our service as leaders within the congregation.

☺ **Reflection Question:** Briefly describe your relationship to your father. What was it when you were growing up? During adolescent years? Adulthood? Now? What *words* could be used to describe your relationship?

Biblical Concept of Father

In the Bible there is more to being a "father" than being a father. When one surveys the use of *father* in either of the Testament, it becomes increasingly apparent that making a singular, definitive, all inclusive portrayal of fatherhood is near to impossible. The word *father* and the father-son imagery are used throughout Scripture to designate a wide variety of things, both literal and figurative.[2] For our purpose, three of its most common uses are most relevant: our literal fathers, God our Father, and our spiritual fathers in the Church.

Most expectedly, the most common or frequent use of *father* in the Bible denotes our physical father, as well as all our ancestors as our "fathers". In fact, Scripture uses the term *father* about our physical male parent long before it ever refers to God as our Father, or introduces the notion of spiritual father.[3] When Moses described God as our Father, he was drawing from the experience the Israelites had with their own fathers. It was if he were saying, "Who is God? He is like your father . . .", invoking a familiar image to explain a theological question. Our relationship with God is to reflect the father-son bond. "Yet to all who received him [Jesus], to those who believed in his name, he gave the right to become *children of God* — children born not of natural descent, nor of human decision or a husband's will, *but born of God*" (John 1:12-13 *emphasis added*). These sentiments are likewise echoed by Paul in Romans when he speak of our spiritual adoption as sons of God (Romans 8:23, 9:4).

However, in the New Testament, the imagery of father was applied to the spiritual lives of mentor-mentoree. For example, Paul refers to himself as the father of the Corinthian congregation (1 Cor. 4:15). Timothy is frequently called a "son" by Paul (Phil. 2:22; 1 Tim. 1:2; 2 Tim. 2:1), even going on to explain that, "But you know that Timothy has proved himself, because as a son with his father he has served with me in the work of the gospel" (Phil. 2:22-23). Paul likewise claimed to be the spiritual father of Titus (Titus 1:4), and even describing Onesimus as, "my son . . . who became my son while I was in chains" (Phm. 10). In some cases, our physical fathers are likewise our spiritual fathers.

How can God, Christian mentors, and most specifically our physical progenitor all be called "father"? It is because of what the Bible describes as the role of father is fulfilled by each of them.[4]

- Fathers have a loving relationship with their children that is readily recognized and experienced (Gen. 37:4; Prov. 3:12, 10:1; Lk. 11:7)
- Fathers nurture and encourage their children (Isa. 1:2; Eph 6:4)
- Fathers give practical life instruction to their children (Gen. 50:16; Prov. 1:8, 6:20; Jer 3:4; Hos. 11:3; 1 Th 2:11)
- Fathers provide corrective guidance and punishment in the context of mercy for their children (Gen. 34:30; Deut. 8:5, 21:18; Ps. 17:25, 27:10, 103:13; 1 Sam. 3:13; Mal. 3:17)

- Fathers provide for their children's needs and wants (Matt. 7:10; Lk. 11:11-13)

How does all this relate to "enjoying fathers"? The concept of "father" in the Bible is far more than just *who* can be identified as a father, or what a father does. It implies a quality of relationship that is shared only between a father and his children. J. Daane perhaps best articulates it:

> Thus the concept of father, whether applied to God, man, the devil, or evil, and whether used biologically or spiritually, literally or figuratively, always expresses the notion of source or fountain of procession. The richness and beauty of the biblical concept of father lies in that, being a source of another, the father imparts and communicates himself to this other. This idea of self-impartation and self-communication is as definitive of the concept of father as is the notion of source. A father gives of himself to that which he fathers, so what proceeds from the source participates in the source. He who is a father communicates something of himself to that which he fathers in such a way that the other has not merely his source in the father, but also the nature of the father's reality. The other partakes of the nature of his father. This accounts for the close ties and deep affection between the source and that which proceeds from it.[5]

However, enjoying the relationship with our fathers does not require them to be the perfect parent or for us to be the perfect son. All of this calls us to recognize our father within us, the legacy he has left us (for good or for ill), and why you are the person you are because of him.

☺**Reflection Question:** As you reflect on Daane's paragraph, how would you compare your idea of "fatherhood" to it? What thoughts does it conger in your mind? Can you think of examples from your father or you as a father that compare to it?

The Legacy of Our Father

We will all leave behind a mixed legacy. Since none of us are perfect, what we bequeath to our sons (and all those with who we are in relation) will be varied. Also, some families are not the iconic traditional family, having suffered the pain of loss from death, divorce, or abandonment; wherein it is possible that as a son you had more than one father who has left an impression upon your life. As a son, you are the recipients of both the shortcomings of your father as well as his strengths; both are his legacy to you.

Sins of the Father

Sometimes, the lessons learned from our father are unfortunate. Intentional or unintentional, the errors of our fathers are part of their legacy. I remember speaking to an elder at a congregation once who's work-ethic was beyond measure. In fact, it began to create family instability, paining his wife and children. I spoke with him about it. He responded, "I work just as hard as my father did. I'm not doing anything different than what he expected of himself." Yes, it was true; but I then asked him, "And how close were you to your father?" He paused, looked down, and eventually said, "Not that close. He was always gone. It was mom who held everything together." Without even realizing it, he was producing the same family dynamic that he was raised in, with the same dysfunctions created by his own father. Regardless of the shortcoming we may have experience, we can still learn from him.

We may perhaps grow up thinking, "I'll never be like that!" and without realizing it, we become it. Remember the cryptic lyric from Harry Chapin's "Cats in the Cradle" (1974):

> I've long since retired, my son's moved away
> I called him up just the other day
> I said, "I'd like to see you if you don't mind"
> He said, "I'd love to, Dad, if I can find the time
> You see my new job's a hassle and kids have the flu
> But it's sure nice talking to you, Dad
> It's been sure nice talking to you"
>
> And as I hung up the phone it occurred to me
> He'd grown up just like me
> My boy was just like me[6]

Acknowledging our father's shortcomings and assessing the mark it left on our lives is the first step at overcoming them. Oftentimes, without realizing it or with the best of intentions, we impress upon our sons our own faults; and as sons we must become aware of the impact our fathers may have had on us. While this may provide an initial reason for behaviors, dispositions, and values; it does not excuse them, only explains them. During the Old Testament's Exilic period (6th century B.C.), the Jews had a popular proverb, "'The fathers have eaten sour grapes, and the children's teeth are set on edge" (Jer. 31:29; Ezek. 18:2). However, God disagrees. He tells His people, "As surely as I live, declares the Sovereign Lord, you will no longer quote this proverb in Israel. For every living soul belongs to me, the father as well as the son — both alike belong to me. The soul who sins is the one who will die" (Ezek. 18:3-4); and "Instead, everyone will die for his own sin; whoever eats sour grapes — his own teeth will be set on edge" (Jer. 31:30). Our fathers may not be perfect, and their sins may have left marks on every dimension of our lives, and it may be easier to blame the failures of our lives on the impressions he has left on us. "The fathers have eaten sour grapes, and the children's teeth are set on edge," but God reminds us that ultimately *we* have free will and *we* are accountable for ourselves. If we recognize the negative impact of a father on our lives, in part or in whole, *we* recognize it and have to address it.

This is easier said than done. Depending on what we are dealing with, it may take more than just realizing the error of our ways and that's it. Granted, we can start by recognizing something that is within us that perhaps doesn't belong to us, something that shouldn't be in our mind or heart. However, we may need to share this with a trusted friend who can provide support, accountability, or perhaps even correction to us. Depending on the severity of the matter, it may require us to come to terms with our fathers through pastoral or even professional counseling. I have met with several men serving in church leadership who have had violent reactions in meetings, to the point of warranting concern from those serving with them. Many of them share instances of physical abuse in their past perpetrated by an angry father, which they now emulate not only in their families, but even in God's family. We must be aware of the sins of our father, and step forward to come to terms with them.

☺**Reflection Question:** Without asking you to be overly critical or forthcoming, what can you acknowledge as a negative part of your father's legacy? What do you have to acknowledge as a shortcoming that has impacted your life and leadership in the church?

Faith of our Fathers

Fathers are not all bad either. Fathers do indeed leave a living faith legacy within us, even after they pass. Sometimes our physical father shares the role of spiritual father as well, and this is perhaps most desirable. If our father was a believer, we can begin to reflect and assess on how he taught us, provided Godly counsel, served as an example, and became our spiritual director from childhood. If our father was not a believer, then we should readily realize the need for us to assume that role with our own children. I remember watching my father faithfully reading the Adult Sunday School Quarterly from Standard Publishing every Saturday night . . . and he wasn't the teacher! He felt as president of his Sunday school class he should simply know what was being taught. (Is it any wonder I went into Christian education?) We are more than willing to ask our sons and daughters, "How was school?", "Do you need money?", "How so-and-so?", or "What do you think you'll be when you grow up?"; but when do we ever ask about their walk with Christ? We make provision for children, for their safety, finances, college plans . . . but when do we intentionally make provision for their faith.

As I reflect on King David, he did indeed leave a mixed faith legacy for his sons. Indeed, his sins were all too frequently reflected in the lives of his own sons and created havoc within his family, in spite of being described as "a man after his own heart" (1 Sam. 13:14b). However, perhaps in one bright shining moment in David's reign was his preparation for the temple's construction. It was David's desire to build a Temple to Yahweh, but he was forbidden to undertake the task. However, David did not simply quit. He made preparation for his son to accomplish it. He gathered the craftsmen, raw materials, and the financial resources necessary for Solomon's success. Hence, when it was time to build the Temple in Jerusalem, Solomon simply had to mobilize the skilled laborers and materials "whom my father David provided" (2 Chron. 2:7). No, our sons will not build a Temple to Yahweh; but what provisions for their faith are you making? How are you preparing them for service in Christ's kingdom in the future? Recognizing our father's faith legacy that is alive within us, and making provision to leave a legacy of faith for our own sons (and daughters) is part of enjoying our fathers and fatherhood.

😊**Reflection Questions:** (1) Can you describe the constructive influence your father has had on your faith? How is his faith reflecting in your life and leadership? (2) What are you doing to pass on your faith, particularly to your sons who may one day serve as elders?

Dealing with the "Ghost" of our Father

"You're not doing it! My father put this very stone in this wall, and you are *not* removing it!" pointing his finger to a rock in a wall in our worship center. Our congregation had experienced growth over the past two years. We were already running double services, but the worship service was becoming increasingly crowded. We had discussed expanding the size of the worship center, but now we hit a roadblock. One of the deacon's fathers had just passed a few weeks earlier. They were particularly close. His father was a charter member of the congregation, and the deacon had been raised in that church since his birth. The notion of removing a wall and moving it was not problem, but removing the wall that had iconic value, one with stones in it that had been placed by the charter members, was too much to even consider. His son was convinced it was his responsibility to make sure his father's legacy was not removed, forgotten, or diminished. There was indeed a "ghost" in the room, "haunting" the decision making process.

Inadvertently, this very loving son was ready to turn the church into a museum, if not a mausoleum. He was in effect haunted by the loss of his father, and wanted to turn the congregation from a missional institution into a museum. We all have the tendency to idealize those whom we lose. At first, this is a natural reaction to losing a father; the desire to preserve his legacy *as it was during his life,* something to be made a memorial to a lost leader . . . his father. However, the best memorial is not a museum, but to continue the work of that individual even during his absence. *Stopping the progress* of what he had dedicated his life to lead is an oxymoron, since it inevitably leads to it's demise. The faith of our fathers should compel us to further adventures in faith for His Kingdom, not making the congregation his memorial.

Enjoying our fathers during time of their loss means fulfilling what they began, not simply preserving what they have done. If the "faith of our fathers" is to live in us beyond the limit of their lives, then we must live a life faithful to the mission of God's kingdom and not simply the memory of our father. Likewise, under some circumstances, it may involve forgiving fathers for their shortcomings and errors. It may well require us to unilaterally forgive the "sins of our father" so we can find closure and move into the future unencumbered by irreconcilable situations. In so doing, we learn to deal constructively with the ghost of our father.

☺ **Reflection Question:** How might you be tempted to allow your allegiance to your father unduly influence your service as a leader? When has the legacy of your father been *more* of an influence than it should be? Can you think of an occasion wherein this occurred?

Son-Father-Grandfather

Enjoying our father does not involve extravagance or even perfection, it simply requires a nurturing relationship that it recognized by him and you. Every father was once a son, and every grandfather was once a son and father. There is a bond in this interrelationship between us all. My father, knowing of my affection for writing instruments, personally selected a pen-set for me as a gift. I have carried those pens with a measured amount of pride as a professor and administrator in several of our higher education institutions. But, let me explain. My father never graduated from high school. Also, the pens themselves . . . they don't really write that well and are indeed not that fashionable. But, that's not the point. They were given to me by my father. That's the point. One day, I will pass them along to one of my children, reminding them of "gramps" and me. More importantly than pens, I want my children to enjoy me as a father, as I have enjoyed my father; to learn from me, and to learn in spite of me, and have a faithful legacy as servants of the church.

☺**Reflection Question:** As a father, what spiritual legacy do you plan to give to your children? How will you begin shaping the faith of the next generation in your family.

Endnotes

---

[1] I want to recognize that we likewise value our relationship with our mothers; but since elders are men, there is a special relationship shared by father-son that later impacts us in adulthood. Hence, the chapter by no means is designed to minimize the influence of mothers or to diminish their impact on our lives; just to address the paternal relationship in the context of elder-leader discussions.

[2] Due to the constraints of chapter length, I cannot provide an exhaustive treatment or word study of *father* here. However, consulting any Bible dictionary or encyclopedia readily demonstrates the wide use of the term, particularly in its figurative sense.

[3] The first reference to "father" in Scripture is in the creation narrative (Genesis 2:24) and throughout Genesis; but the first depiction of God as "father" is implied in Exodus 4:22 and stated in Deuteronomy 32:6. While both were written by the prophet Moses around 1500B.C., the time span between creation and the actual events of Moses' life is inestimable.

[4] The following section is based on information gleaned from Philip Wendell Crannell "Father," *International Standard Bible Encyclopaedia*, Electronic Database, 1996, 2003, 2006 by Biblesoft, Inc. in PC Study Bible V5.

[5] J. Daane, "Father," *International Standard Bible Encyclopedia*, Revised Edition (Grand Rapids: Eerdmans Publishing, 1979) in PC Study Bible V5.

[6] Lyrics from www.lyricsdepot.com.

Chapter 3

Enjoying Friendships with Those in the Faith

David Roadcup

"How good and pleasant it is when brothers live together in unity."
Psalms 133:2

"We are all angels with only one wing; we can only fly while embracing one another."
Luciano De Crescenzo

Developing the ability to build and maintain good friendships and relationships with those inside the church is of utmost importance for an effective elder. This aspect of an elder's role is the *foundation* for almost all of the other responsibilities he must carry.

One of the most enjoyable parts of being a member of the body of Christ is the nurturing relationships we can form over the months and years. We encounter people whom we truly love and care about when the church meets in our large worship group or small home group during the week. We connect with people who are truly genuine, loving, mature and supportive and who demonstrate these characteristics to us in significant friendships. It is what God intended for us to experience and enjoy as we become part of the living, breathing body of Christ.

God's will is clear in Scripture when it comes to the topic of friendship and relationships in the body of Christ whether we are elders or members of the church. When we think about the will of God, there are two aspects of His will that are important to consider. The first is what is referred to as the *universal* will of God. This is God's will revealed in Scripture that is true for all mankind in all situations in all generations. That God would see all men come to salvation is clear from John 3:16. That will never change. God's call to Christ followers to be people of integrity and personal purity will always be God's will. The sanctity of marriage in any culture will always be God's will. Specific concepts and commands that do not change, that can be studied and understood from the Word of God come under the concept of the *universal* will of God. The other category concerning the will of God is called the *specific* will of God. The *specific* will of God is God's will for each person in their individual lives, spiritual journeys, family and work. Who we will marry, where we will work and other specific details of our lives and how they unfold come under the *specific* will of God for us.

When we discuss friendship and relationship building for elders in the church, both the universal and specific will of God are clear about what God had planned and intended. His heart for all believers is that they develop a mature, loving and specific commitment to each other as members of the Body of Christ. "Christian brotherhood is not an ideal which we must realize; it is rather a reality created by God in Christ in which we may participate."[1]

Lynn Anderson, in his excellent book *They Smell Like Sheep Volume 2*, states, "God's number one priority is *people*. God who is in 'the people business,' has also called us into people-centered living. Thus, the most God-like thing a shepherd can do is to give people the priority God gives us and to treat people the way Jesus did."[2]

God calls all elders to become involved with the sheep of the church. There are several critical roles that an elder must fulfill, but none more important than building relationships with the believers in his flock. Elders lead the way here as they model this Biblical imperative.

When we are discussing the great importance of friendship and relationships in the life of believers, especially the elder team of a congregation, the point is doubly true. Elders in the church need to work hard at loving the members of the body and building relationships with those who may come into their relational web. It is obvious that developing the ability to build and maintain good relationships with those inside the church is of utmost importance for an effective elder. It is not an option for an elder leader. It is vital and a big part of an effective elder's work.

☺**Reflection Question:** Who are your "closest" friends? Are they from the church? Work? Neighborhood? Is there a reason your closest friends are (or are not) in the church?

The actual size of a congregation will have a lot to do with how extensive an elder's network of relationships can be. But whatever the size of the congregation -- whether a small church of fifty or less, a mid-sized church of two to three hundred, or all the way to a large mega-church in the thousands -- elders must develop and maintain quality relationships with their people.

Scripture Teaches Us about Friendship and Relationships

An important issue to keep in mind at all times is, "What is God's heart about this topic? What does God want to see happen here?" In light of that fact, we need to examine Scripture and see what the Lord teaches us and what He wants.

Jesus' Teachings - Jesus our Lord taught many things about friendship and relationships. One of his most poignant teachings about our relationships in the church comes in John 15. In verses 12-13, Jesus states, "My command is this: love each other as I have loved you. Greater love has no one than this, that he lay down his life for his friends." In verse 17 he repeats, "This is my command: Love each other."

How do you command someone to love another? Is it possible? To understand how Jesus can give us this directive, we must go to the background of the word Jesus used in these verses. The word that Jesus uses is the Greek word, *agape*. Agape is a type of love that primarily comes from the intellect and mind as opposed to coming from the heart or emotions. It is a kind of love that is mature, responsible and intensely committed. It may have emotional aspects to it or emotion may not be involved. The central meaning of the word is that we have an intellectual commitment and connection to someone for their good, our good and the good of the church. That's how Jesus can command us to love each other. We do this by an act of our will much more than a reaction from our emotions.

The main point is this – it is the heart of Jesus that genuine and authentic love be a major part of our relationships within the church. Elders need to lead the way when it comes loving each other as members of the body of Christ. A loving elder is an effective elder. A loving elder changes, builds and blesses people's lives.

Paul's Teachings - The apostle Paul supports Jesus' imperative. All through his communication to the churches, Paul emphasizes the overriding importance of genuine friendships and relationship building. Paul models this as he writes to the Philippians in chapter 1 verse 7, "It is right for me to feel this way about all of you, since I have you in my heart; for whether I am in chains or defending and confirming the gospel, all of you share in God's grace with me. God can testify how I long for all of you with the affection of Jesus Christ." Concerning love between fellow believers, Paul states in 2 Thessalonians 1: 3, "We ought always to thank God for you, brothers, and rightly so, because your faith is growing more and more, and the love every one of you has for each other is increasing." Whether we read 1 Corinthians 13, Romans 12:10, Colossians 3:12-13, 1 Thessalonians 4: 9-10 or many other references, we see clearly that a major value of Paul was to encourage believers in their love and devotion for each other. This is clearly part of the will of our Father as we live together and work together as the body of Christ.

Peter's Teachings -   Peter continues to teach us about loving relationships. Peter had been with Jesus and knew clearly what relationships should look like between those in God's family. He teaches us in 1 Peter 1:22-23, "Now that you have purified yourselves by obeying the truth so that you have sincere love for your brothers, love one another deeply, from the heart. For you have been born again, not of perishable seed, but of imperishable, through the living and enduring word of God." Peter also exhorts us in 1 Peter 2:17, "Love the brotherhood of believers…" and in 5:14, "Greet one another with a kiss of love."

The doctrine of loving one another and building and maintaining relationships with one another as believers in the body of Christ cannot be more clearly stated. We know God's heart in this area. The scripture references noted here are just a sampling of the numerous teachings from the Word. The Lord shows us his heart in scripture when it comes to elder/leaders in the church, loving and caring for our flock.

☺**Reflection Question:**   How do your church relationships demonstrate a biblical love for those in the faith? What might be an area for improvement that is needed? How would you start making this improvement?

In the teachings of the New Testament, there are numerous places where writers admonish us to build relationships. These places are called the *"one another"* passages. Below is a list of many of these references:

1. Be at peace with one another (Mark 9:50)	15. Speak to one another with psalms, hymns and spiritual songs (Ephesians 5:19)
2. Love one another (John 13:34)	
3. Be devoted to one another (Romans 12:10)	16. Submit to one another out of reverence for Christ (Ephesians 5:21)
4. Honor one another (Romans 12:10)	
5. Live in harmony with one another (Romans 12:16)	17. In humility consider others better than yourselves (Philippians 2:3)
6. Stop passing judgment on one another (Romans 14:13)	18. Teach one another (Colossians 3:16)
7. Accept one another (Romans 15:7)	19. Admonish one another (Colossians 3:16)
8. Instruct one another (Romans 15:14)	20. Encourage each other (1 Thessalonians 4:18)
9. Greet one another (Romans 16:16)	21. Build each other up (1 Thessalonians 5:11)
10. Serve one another (Galatians 5:13)	22. Spur one another on toward love and good deeds (Hebrews 10:24)
11. Carry each other's burden (Galatians 6:2)	23. Do not slander one another (James 4:11)
12. Be patient, bearing with one another in love (Ephesians 4:2)	24. Don't grumble against each other (James 5:9)
13. Be kind and compassionate to one another (Ephesians 4:32)	25. Confess your sins to each other (James 5:16)
14. Forgive each other (Ephesians 4:32)	26. Pray for one another (James 5:16)
	27. Clothe yourselves with humility toward one another (1 Peter 5:5)

☺**Reflection Question:** Given the rather exhaustive list above, which are the top three ways you exemplify the "one another" principle in your life? What might be the "bottom" three ways you need to work on in your relationships?

Levels of Relationship

Norman Wright, a relationship expert, tells us in his book titled, *Relationships That Work*, that there are four basic levels of relationship. First, there are *minimal* relationships. These are relationships that are surface but tend to be pleasant. At this level, little help or emotional support is extended. People communicate pleasantly and acknowledge each other. Passing those in the hallway or in the parking lot on Sundays that we know on a very surface level would fit this category. Second, there are *moderate* relationships. "A moderate relationship has all the characteristics of a minimal relationship, but includes one more: an emotional attachment."[3] In moderate relationships, we listen to each other's joys and struggles and exchange mutual support. The third relationship level is called the *strong* relationship. "The difference between a moderate relationship and a strong one is found in one simple word - *help*. Strong relationships develop when you have high involvement with people. You do this by reaching out to minister to them in tangible ways. You're ready to provide help when they need it. You also accept help from them when you need it."[4] Fourth, *quality* relationships are the deepest kind of relationships. This level includes the aspect of loving trust. We have the ability to open our interior worlds to this group and trust them in doing so. They share deeper things with us. Our transparency and trust together produce a deep level of connection.

As elders, there are people in our relational web at all of the above mentioned levels. There are those in the church we know casually. There are those we are closer to in terms of emotional attachment, possibly in our Sunday School class or Adult Bible Fellowship. There are people we feel we could ask for help if we needed to. And there are those who are close, personal friends who are in the *quality* relationship level such as fellow elders or those in our small home bible study group. Being aware of these levels will help relate to each group carefully and assist us in connecting as effectively as possible.

☺Reflection Question: How do having "quality" relationships in the church aid you in serving as an elder? How could their absence hinder your leadership? What can you do to build quality relationships with others in your congregation?

Building and Maintaining Healthy Relationships

Through many years of research in the human sciences, the key aspects of building and maintaining friendships and relationships are identifiable and clear. They are discussed in Scripture as well as in the literature in the field of human science. Listed below are the basic keys to reaching out and developing solid relationships and friendship:

1. *Proactively reaching out* – Building and maintaining relationships takes intentionality! It takes personal initiative on the part of the elder to build relationships. Friendships take work, cultivation and care. For extroverts, this step is natural. For introverts, it may take risk and the expending of oneself. An elder/leader will put forth the effort to reach out and be the first one to extend a hand, an invitation to lunch or to a small group.

2. *Time* – For people in many of today's world cultures, time is the new currency. Many leaders live an intense, pressure cooker, helter-skelter lifestyle. Time is always in short supply. Where time is spent is an important priority. As an elder in the church, deciding to use time from your busy schedule to connect to people is an important decision. Relationships are always forged in the crucible of time. Spending time together allows people to get to know each other and facilitates the growth of that friendship. Time is the medium. In

many cases, the more time you spend with someone, the more the relationship will grow.

3. *Personal attention* – Committing personal attention to others always communicates the desire to connect. When we give attention to people, we are saying, "You are important to me and worthy of one of my most prized possessions, the possession of time." We give attention to people by connecting with them, asking about their lives and participating in their life experiences.

4. *Communication* – The heart of any relationship is communication. From pleasant social conversation before and after church services to a time of personal, transparent sharing over a meal, any good friendship is built on two or more people talking, thinking and feeling together as a relationship deepens. Communication is the life's blood to people growing together. Relationships at any level cannot flourish without this important element.

5. *Transparency* – In communication, the issue of being transparent is an important part of that process. Amongst the different levels of communication, the deepest and most meaningful are those in which the participants involved, over time and through the building of trust, can open up and share some of what is happening in their interior world.

6. *The giving and receiving of gifts* – For thousands of years, the giving and receiving of gifts has been a meaningful part of communicating the desire to build a relationship. The giving of a gift says, "You are important to me and I had you in my thoughts." Gifts do not have to be large or expensive to be meaningful. A gift of food or personal item can carry an important message of acceptance and affection.

7. *Kind words* –Robert Schuller has commented on kind words. "I am convinced that words have enormous power. They are either bombs or balms. They level us or they can lift us. They carry with them power to connect with the memory system that can release

healing powers or destructive powers."[5] An elder who knows how to encourage, support and build up people through his words will bless the members of his congregation. Kind words are very powerful in the lives of the people in our church because there is a real dearth of kindness, encouragement and support in most people's worlds, in general. When genuine kindness and concern is delivered through our words, it impacts people's lives.

   8. *Acts of love and service* – When desiring to build a relationship, performing caring acts of love and service to our sheep are powerful in their impact. It can be helping with a task (light car maintenance or painting a room together, etc.) Acts of love can be expressed at difficult times of our lives, as well. An elder and his

wife from Texas led a small home Bible study group in their home. They came to love the members of their group as the months passed. One of the men in the group did not have a positive relationship with his father who lived several states away. The father suddenly died and the son, the member of the elder's group, traveled to the funeral. In his own words, "Not many people showed up for my dad's visitation. But then, at just the right time, a very familiar face walked through the doors. It was a Texas shepherd – and one of my best friends- who had dropped me off at the Dallas airport. His presence seized my heart, helped me breath full breaths again. I didn't realize how much I needed him til I saw him. He stayed less than twenty-four hours. I don't know why I felt so surprised – it is who he is. It was an extraordinary moment of shepherding. As I told him, 'Thanks for coming' he said, 'I just had to come. Someone from home needed to be here.' Whew! I breathed deeply again, felt friendship and love fill my eyes, and thanked God for the heart of a shepherd."[6]

9. *Dependability* - A mature part of building relationships can be seen in the quality of *dependability*. Just being dependable. Just following through. Whether it is arriving on time for a lunch or meeting or delivering on a promise made, doing what you say you are going to do and following through is crucial in friendship building.

10. *Careful listening* – Paul Tillich, the famous psychologist has written, "The first duty of love is to listen."[7] Listening is a powerful friendship building tool. It communicates interest and genuine concern. When we take the time to carefully listen to someone and invest ourselves in their interests and concerns, it is a gift to them. Effective listening is a bridge building ministry to others.

11. *Loyalty* – In I Samuel, the story of the relationship between David and Jonathan is exemplary. Through severe trials brought about by King Saul, David and Jonathan maintained their relationship. Jonathan's loyalty to David is striking. It should be the same between brothers (and sisters) in Christ, especially leaders. The level of loyalty should be committed and solid. We build our relationship and then we stand together, back to back, through all circumstances.

These actions and others are the keys to beginning, growing and maintaining relationships. With these abilities, elders should be able to minister to individuals effectively when it comes to friendships in their ministries.

☺**Reflection Question:** Based on the previous eleven items, rate on a scale of 1-5, one being low and 5 being high, your qualities as a friend.

Proactively Reaching	① ② ③ ④ ⑤	Kind Words	① ② ③ ④ ⑤
Time	① ② ③ ④ ⑤	Acts of Love & Service	① ② ③ ④ ⑤
Personal Attention	① ② ③ ④ ⑤	Dependability	① ② ③ ④ ⑤
Communication	① ② ③ ④ ⑤	Carefully Listen	① ② ③ ④ ⑤

Transparency	①②③④⑤	Loyalty	①②③④⑤
Give/Receive Gifts	①②③④⑤	*OVERALL?*	①②③④⑤

An Elder's Relationships in the Church

Let's now identify the specific groups of people with whom an elder might connect when it comes to relationships within the church:

Fellow Elders

There should be strong camaraderie, support, love and unity within every eldership team. Every elder on the team should look at every other elder as he would a blood brother. There can be strong personalities on an eldership. That can be a real plus. Many primary leaders are men who are focused, confident and talented. And in the midst of a group of strong leaders, there should always be a spirit of grace, forbearance and humility. As an elder, we are always ready to "give preference to one another in honor." As leaders, we are always part of the relational solution, never part of the problem. If an elder brother is not following the Lord's will in this area, he should be called out and asked to repent. Remember, one selfish, egotistical, power hungry elder can negatively affect the entire eldership.

It definitely strengthens the relational web that elders should share by spending time together outside formal meetings. Getting together with our wives (and families) for meals and other informal activities can help us to get to know each other at levels that attending meetings cannot. How about after worship services for lunch or a meal? We have to eat meals anyway. Why not spend that time together? Going to a sports event, concert or having a picnic together will serve to strengthen our ties and bring us closer together. In one of my preaching ministries, our elder team met once a month for a year to have dinner in each other's homes. We took turns hosting the group. Everyone brought something for the dinner. We did no business. We met, enjoyed dinner, talked and laughed together and closed with a solid prayer time. These times together were great for the bonding that needed to happen with that group of men and their wives.

It is also crucial to have at least one retreat a year together as the elder team and staff. Choosing a Friday evening and Saturday to get away for study, prayer, planning, evaluation and relationship building is a very worthy investment for any eldership to make.[8]

The Paid Staff

It goes without saying that the relationship between the members of the elder team and the paid staff is crucial. Since these are the two major groups providing leadership and direction for the congregation, their unity and love for each other is of *utmost importance*. The paid staff and elder team must be one in heart and spirit as they lead the church to fulfill its mission.

Possibly one of the most significant accounts in all of the N.T. about leadership relationships come in Acts 20:17-38. Paul is on his way by ship to Jerusalem to celebrate the day of Pentecost. He stops in Miletus and calls for the elders of the church in Ephesus. Paul probably planted the church in Ephesus and had many close relationships there. He may have won to Christ and discipled many of the elders who came to Miletus to see him. When they arrived, he talked to them about his ministry with them. He told them he was on his way to Jerusalem and that after this visit, he would not see them again. He encouraged them to "guard the flock" and commended them to the Lord. They knelt down on the seashore and prayed together. Verses 37-38 tell us, "They all wept as they embraced him and kissed him. What grieved them the most was his statement that they would never see his face again. Then they accompanied him to the ship." If we think of Paul as the preaching minister of the church in Ephesus, this is a picture of mutual love and commitment which provides the model to us for the kind of relationship elder teams and paid staff should have. We are brothers – washed in the blood of Christ and children of the Great King. In this story, there is warmth, concern, care and encouragement for each other. There is honor and respect. Prayer together was a part of this relationship. What an excellent model of heart-felt coming together between staff and elders! Our prayer should be that all church leadership teams would relate to each other on this level.

In many cases, however, this is not the model. In some staff/elder relationships, communication has broken down, misunderstandings have arisen and there is anger, distrust, serious disagreement and hurt feelings. This always results in a breakdown of unity and cohesiveness. There are struggles and arguments over power, control and the direction of the church. This absolutely should not happen in the leadership team of the body of Christ! Not only is this relational activity against the heart and will of God but the church is almost always *aware* that this is the case. The result is that the very men who are to be examples and models to the congregation of unity, love, patience and grace are just the opposite of what they are supposed to represent. The elders and staff must work together, communicate, discuss problems and work out successful solutions.

Paul writes about the attitude that we should have between each other as leaders in the church when he states, "Do not rebuke an older man harshly, but exhort him as if he were your father. Treat younger men as brothers, older women as mothers, and younger women as sisters, with absolute purity." (I Tim. 5:1) In other words, as leaders in the church, the younger men are to respect the older men as their fathers, their peers as their brothers and we could say the younger men as younger brothers. In like response, the older men are to treat the younger men as their sons and their peers as brothers. Older men are to be treated as grandfathers. Respect, honor, love, forgiveness and patience should always govern our relationships in the Lord.

A larger church in the Midwest has a great plan for coupling elders and staff with excellent results. Every staff member has an elder and others (four or five total) who are his/her accountability team. (Many of the teams are made up of people who manage people at work or who have the relational skills to naturally connect with people.) The accountability team meets monthly with the staff member for breakfast or lunch. The purpose of this meeting is to check in with the staff member to see how their ministries, families and lives in general are going. The lunch or breakfast is filled with conversation, support, love and communication. If there is a problem with the staff member or his/her performance or ministry, the accountability team is the first group to address that issue with the staff member. Staff members at this church have told me how much they appreciate the communication and support which comes from their accountability team. The accountability team is a great tool to connect with and support each paid staff member. This plan is workable with large or small churches, either one.

When it comes to elders dealing with staff members (especially those who are young and growing in experience), it is important to remember this dictum: Treat staff members like you would like to have your son or daughter treated if they were in ministry. This applies to salary, communication and loving concern in every situation. Paid staff members should honor and respect men who lead as elders.

If there is ever a problem or relational pothole in your dealings with staff or fellow elders, do what Jesus requested in Matt. 18:15-17. After prayer, go to him/her immediately with a spirit of humility, having bathed the situation in prayer and talk about the problem, offense or misunderstanding. This can resolve many problems quickly through a loving spirit and communication. Be quick to forgive and never carry anger or a grudge towards a brother or sister in Christ.

Sunday School or Adult Bible Fellowship

Whatever its name, if your congregation has a learning or content time before or after the worship service, elders can maximize their impact by being active in a class or group. Strong relationships are created in mid-sized groups. Elders can teach and model for their group members powerful lessons for successfully living and growing in Christ. By teaching or attending, it is a great way to significantly connect with a segment of the church's population.

The Elder's Small Group

Every elder should participate in the small group ministry of his congregation. It is important for every congregation to have an effective small groups ministry. Primarily because small groups is, without question, the finest approach to shepherding found to date. There is nothing more effective. Emphasis should be placed on the word, *effective*. There are small group ministries which do very little for a congregation and eventually burnout. But an effective small groups ministry which is carefully managed and well led will provide an approach to shepherding people that is unmatched with any other approach. Because of the shepherding effectiveness of small groups, elders should be a part of that ministry. Whether leading a group or being an active participant, the presence of elders in the small group ministry is impacting and absolutely necessary.

The Congregation at Large

In churches that average below 100 in attendance, it is not hard to have a working knowledge of most of the people who attend. As the number of attendees goes up, being able to know people gets more difficult. In churches of 500 plus, it is very possible to not know many of the regular attendees. In mega-churches that run in the thousands, it may be possible to not know a large number of attendees. So, how does an effective elder shepherd in larger or mega-church situations? There are several suggestions.

- Elders can position themselves before and after services to simply greet people in the foyer as they are coming and going. Many church members of larger churches state that they do not know who the elders of their congregation are due to the size of the church. Over the course of time, elders could connect with a meaningful segment of the congregation, simply through their visibility before and after services in the foyer.
- After every Saturday evening service and the several services on Sunday morning, one large congregation in Indiana announces that after the services, several of the elders will be "down front" and available for prayer, questions or conversation. Many people connect with the eldership of this mega-church through contact with the elders at the end of services.
- Elders can make an effort to get to know as many people as possible through short term mission trips, ministry team meetings, men's ministry events and retreats, etc. Just being aware of those whom we have the chance to be around, getting their names, etc. can be helpful.

☺Reflection Question: Of the groups/individuals mentioned above, which one are you most comfortable relating too? Which one(s) present a challenge? Explain your responses and try to give examples.

Conclusion

One of the most significant aspects of the work of the elder is connecting with people. It is proactively reaching out to people, taking time for them, developing relationships to them and being aware of the fact that God has called us to make this our primary mission. People are the reason why Jesus came. People are the reason there is a heaven being prepared for each of us, even as you are reading this chapter. As we shepherd in the body of Christ, as we enjoy our flock, let us do all we can to make sure, through our watch-care, that as many people as possible will be there.

📖 Resources for Elder Relationships

- *Built to Last* by Kenneth Hagin Jr. (Standard Publishing Co., 2002)
- *Love: Building Healthy Relationships, Fruit of the Spirit Bible Studies* by Peter Scazzero (Zondervan, 2001)
- *Why You Do the Things You Do: The Secret to Healthy Relationships* by Tim Clinton, Dr. Gary Sibcy (Thomas Nelson, 2006)
- *Relationships 101* by John C. Maxwell (Thomas Nelson, 2003)
- *The Five Languages of Apology: How to Experience Healing in All Your Relationships* by Gary Chapman and Jennifer Thomason (Thomas Nelson, 2008)
- *Listening to the Other: A Practical Approach to Listening Skills* by Caroline Blazier (John Hunt Pub. 2009)
- *Getting along with people you love: Building and maintaining healthy relationships* (Growing together studies) by Marlin Moraves
- *Authentic Relationships: Discover the Lost Art of One Anothering* by: Wayne Jacobsen, Clay Jacobsen Baker / 2003
- "Building Healthy Relationships," September 10th, 2007 by Tejyan Pettinger; www.pickthebrain.com/blog/build-healthy-relationships/

Endnotes

[1] Dietrich Bonhoeffer, Life Together (New York: Harper and Row, 1954) 30.

[2] Lynn Anderson, *They Smell Like Sheep Volume 2* (New York: Simon and Schuster, 2007) 97-98.

[3] H. Norman Wright, *Relationships That Work* (Ventura: Regal Books, 1998) 15.

[4] Ibid., 16.

[5] Website: http://www.wordscanheal.com/aboutus/endorsements.

[6] Lynn Anderson, *They Smell Like Sheep Volume 2* (New York: Simon and Schuster, 2007) 101.

[7] Alan Loy McGinnis, *The Friendship Factor* (Minneapolis: Augsburg, 1979) 109.

[8] For an excellent schedule of events for an elder's retreat, see *The Biblical Role of Elders for Today's Church* by Kreider, Myer, Prokopchak and Sauder, House To House Publications, 2004, pages 105-106 for good ideas and schedule.

Chapter 4

Enjoying...Those Not of the Faith

Gary L. Johnson

"The Church is like manure. Pile it up,
and it stinks up the neighborhood; spread it out,
and it enriches the world."
Luis Palau

Countless people are in need of Christ, and Jesus is counting on countless Christians to reach those who are spiritually lost. We have been given a mandate by Jesus Christ, Himself, to "make disciples of all nations," and that mandate will always be in effect. The question is, "Will we be effective in fulfilling the mandate?"

Regretfully, Christians have been negligent in sharing Christ with those who are outside of Christ. Over the years, we have developed a "Little Bo Peep mentality." Do you remember that nursery rhyme? "Little Bo Peep has lost her sheep and can't tell where to find them. Leave them alone, they'll come home, wagging their tails behind them." Too many of us are waiting for the lost to find their own way "home" to Christ. We are waiting for the lost to just show up in church so that they can hear the good news about Jesus Christ. This mentality does not work, and it will never work.

If the local church is to "make disciples of every nation," it will be necessary for Christians to be taught how to bring people to Christ. Logically, the spiritual leaders should be teaching the people how to do just that by their example. Again, that is not happening, and it is regretful. Dr. Thom Rainer, a noted writer and researcher regarding the American Church substantiates this fact.

Church leaders are becoming less evangelistic. A survey of pastors I led in 2005 surprised the research team. Over one-half (53%) of pastors have made no evangelistic efforts at all in the past six months. They have not shared the Gospel. They have not attempted to engage a lost and unchurched person at any level.[1]

If our spiritual leaders are not leading people to Christ, we should not expect the typical church member to be doing so. Moreover, not only are fewer Christians making an effort to bring people to Christ, there are fewer Christians in the church. We tend to think that the unsaved are those of other world religions (i.e., Islam, Buddhism, Hinduism, etc.), but there are vast numbers of protestants who are dying without Christ because they have not surrendered their lives to Him. There are far too many people warming the pews of churches who are not authentic followers of Jesus Christ; they merely go through the motions. These individuals need to be brought to Christ through intra-evangelism—a term meaning to evangelize those inside the church.

The task before us is beyond enormous. For us to pursue the mandate of making disciples of all nations, we must have the desire to do so. A classic movie from years past is *The Wizard of Oz*. In it, Dorothy meets three new friends while walking on the yellow brick road: a scarecrow that needed a brain, a tin man who needed a heart, and a lion that needed courage. In each of these instances, we discover three reasons why we fail to share our faith with the lost. Like the scarecrow, we think we do not know enough. Like the lion, we fear rejection or failure, and so we lack courage. Like the tin man, we do not have a heart for the lost—we simply do not care about them.

Something has to change. As leaders of the church, we need to come to grips with this pivotal issue. As elders, are we reaching out to the lost? When was the last time you shared your faith with an individual and led that person to Christ? Do you remember the name of that individual? Did you baptize that person into Christ? One last question: do you know how to lead a person to Christ? The issue is not simply that we are not leading people to Christ; the fact of the matter is that many elders do not know how to bring a person to Christ.

☺Reflection Question: Name the person to whom you most recently presented the gospel. Name the person, a non-Christian, who you last brought to church with you. To whom did you last share your testimony about Christ?

Evangelism 101

The following is an explanation that I have used literally hundreds of times in sharing the Gospel with people who are not followers of Christ. This same explanation was shared with me in 1978, and once I heard the way to Christ explained in this manner, I immediately received Christ and was baptized into Jesus that very night. As I describe this process to you, I have included a diagram of six circles that I draw while explaining the gospel to an individual. Please keep referring to the diagram, and imagine yourself drawing it out while sharing your faith. It is important that we know how to confidently share the gospel because it is becoming increasingly difficult to bring people to Christ for two simple reasons: 1) anti-Christian sentiment is becoming progressively worse, and 2) with fewer people becoming saved, a person cannot introduce another individual to Jesus Christ, who they do not know.

Become familiar with the following. Study it, and then practice it with your spouse, your children, even your fellow elders. Learn how to share your faith and ache to bring another person to Christ. A male octopus will mate once in its lifetime and then swim off and die.

The female octopus will give birth to her young, nourish them with food, and then the female also dies. The young even feed from her carcass. A male and female octopus has a desire to reproduce at least once in its lifetime and then dies. Can we say the same spiritually? Do we desire to bring at least one individual to Christ, baptizing them in the faith and discipling them into Christ prior to our death? This must be our desire. Read on.

The Six Circles Diagram

On a piece of paper, draw six circles at what would be the numbers 12, 2, 4, 6, 8 and 10 on the face of a clock. Using <u>six circles</u>, please follow the flow of the diagram and the logic of Scripture in reaching heaven.

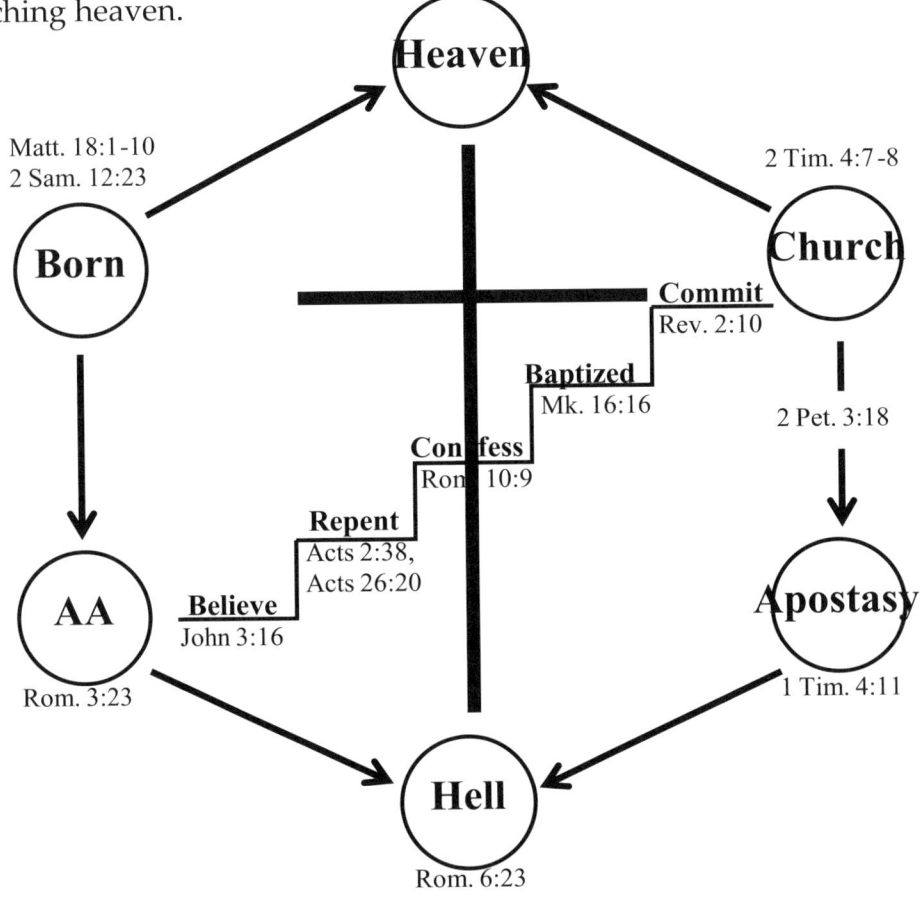

First, we believe there is a literal heaven and hell because the Bible teaches authoritatively such truth (see top and bottom circles). These are places that exist beyond this realm of reality. The reality of heaven and hell have been substantiated by medical science and its ability to resuscitate people from being pronounced clinically dead, and their immediate comments are descriptive of an afterlife—some experiences being pleasant, and some not-so-pleasant. Dr. Maurice Rawlings, in his book *Beyond Death's Door*, details how people describe the next realm of existence after having been resuscitated in trauma units. After listening to literally hundreds of such patients, Rawlings is convinced that there is a realm "beyond death's door", one that is indescribably pleasant and one that is indescribably painful.

We begin our journey in life by being physically born (top left-side circle). Should a child die, that little one is ushered into the very presence of God in heaven. Why? The child is morally innocent, he or she is without sin. Hell is a place of punishment for our sins. Sin is to be in opposition against God. A little child is not capable of opposing God by rebelling against Him. Should a child die, the child is morally innocent and is immediately in paradise (i.e., heaven). Moreover, when someone states that the child is condemned to hell for the sin of the parent(s), we must remember that Ezekiel 18:20 states that we are individually responsible for our sins. When King David grieved the death of his child born to him as a result of committing adultery with Bathsheba, David said that the child would not "come to me, but I will go to the child" (see 2 Samuel 12:23), meaning that the child had died and returned to God, the Giver of life. In turn, David would someday die and return to God. Finally, we must emphasize that Jesus had a great heart for little children, and we can rest assured that the compassion of Jesus Christ would extend to morally innocent little ones (see Matthew 18:1-10, Mark 10:13-16).

Yet, for the most part, people grow up and reach the age of accountability (see bottom left-side circle). This is not a set chronological age for all people. It is reached at various times in people's lives when the individual recognizes there is a difference between moral right and wrong. The person will have an understanding that "all have sinned and fallen short of the glory of God" (see Romans 3:23). So, a person who grows up in a "Jesus-rich" environment will experience a sense of being held accountable for sin at a much earlier age than a person who grows up with little exposure to Christianity.

It is at this moment in life when the person realizes that there are consequences for his or her actions. If the individual does not acknowledge God and rejects a relationship with Jesus Christ as Lord and Savior, and should the individual die, hell is experienced (see bottom circle), for "the wages of sin is death" (Rom. 6:23). But, rather than focus on the bad news, let's focus on the good news in that Jesus Christ is "the way, the truth, and the life" in order for us to be restored to God, our Creator (see John 14:6).

Looking at the center of the circles, a cross can be drawn to represent thje way an individual goes through Jesus Christ to be restored to God in heaven. Beginning at the circle marked "age of accountability," we can draw a set of stairs to represent the path by which we are led to God by salvation in Christ. On the first step, we begin with belief. It is essential to believe in Jesus Christ (see John 3:16). The phrase "whosoever believes" John 3:16 means that an individual continues in belief as the word "believes" is in the present tense of Greek, meaning the action of belief continues and does not cease. Belief in Jesus Christ is foundational to a relationship with God. Just as we begin building a house by laying the foundation, we begin building a relationship with God by laying a foundation of belief in Christ.

Next, moving up the stairs, we find that it is essential to <u>repent</u> of our sins (see Acts 2:38, Acts 26:20). Repentance was an important element in the preaching ministry of Jesus Christ. Like two book ends, the ministry of Jesus is marked with preaching repentance at both its beginning and end (see Matthew 4:17 and Luke 24:47). Repentance is not living a perfect life morally, but it is a changed life spiritually. We are to "hunger and thirst after righteousness" (see Matthew 5:6), which means that we are to have an "appetite" for holiness. That happens when we have a change of attitude from having a change in our thinking. Repent is the word *metanoia* in Greek, which is a compound word of *meta* (meaning change) and *noia* (meaning mind). Hence, if we "change our minds (i.e., change the way we think), there is greater likelihood of changing the way we act. Ergo, we repent. This is a deliberate decision and act of the will that is essential in the process of coming to God.

As we move along this "stairway to heaven," we discover that it is essential to make what is called the good <u>confession</u> (i.e., go public with one's decision to be a Christian). This is articulated well in Romans 10:9, in that if we <u>believe</u> in our hearts that God raised Jesus from the dead, and we <u>confess</u> with our mouths that Jesus is Lord, we will be saved. In Matthew 10:32-33, Jesus said He will acknowledge us before His Father in heaven if we acknowledge Him before others. We cannot be ashamed of Jesus Christ! Once we make a public decision for Christ, such as during an altar call at the conclusion of a worship service, it is not a "one time" moment of going public with one's faith. We believe that a person must be ready and willing to admit in many settings that one is a Christian (i.e., at school, in a family setting, at work, etc.).

<u>Baptism</u> is yet another important moment in one's spiritual journey of salvation. There are many verses that make mention of

baptism in the New Testament. For example, Jesus said that whoever believes and is baptized will be saved (see Mark 16:16). Paul mentioned that baptism is a "burial" of our old self and we are raised to a new life in Christ (see Romans 6:1-4, Colossians 2:12). As well, Jesus Himself instituted this sacrament when He was baptized (see Matthew 3:13-17). Baptism is not to be interpreted as something we do to earn our salvation. When a person is being baptized, he or she is not doing anything. Rather, the individual is allowing something to be done to him or to her. This is seen in the passive voice of the word "baptize" -- passive meaning to allow something to be done to you.

Also, it is important to note who is a candidate to be baptized. Jesus said whoever believes <u>and</u> is baptized will be saved. This indicates that the individual should have the ability to mentally believe in the person of Jesus Christ. Moreover, Acts 2:38 states that we are to repent and be baptized to receive the gift of the Holy Spirit and for our sins to be forgiven. So then, a candidate to be baptized must have the ability to repent (i.e., "change the mind" and behavior). This clearly indicates that infants and toddlers are not candidates for baptism. Infant baptism and infant sprinkling came into vogue long after the early Church was established.

The mode of baptism expanded to include infant or adult sprinkling (Greek *rantidzo*), pouring (Greek *ekcheo*), or immersion (Greek *baptidzo*). Yet, only *baptidzo* appears in the Greek New Testament manuscript, even though both *ekcheo* and *rantidzo* were available in the first century Greek vocabulary. Also, our Bibles use a transliteration of the word "baptism" when the Greek word in the text means literally "immerse or dip." Acts 2:38 literally reads, "Repent and be immersed..." The use of the transliteration allows people to define the mode of baptism according to their wishes, even though the Greek word means to immerse. If

there were other forms of baptism practiced in the first century church, it is reasonable to think that such terminology would appear in the New Testament. Moreover, only immersion "fits" the Biblical imagery of going down into the water, coming up out of the water, being buried (see Romans 6:4, Colossians 2:12). Keep in mind that baptism is a sacrament that reminds us visually that Jesus died for our sins and was raised from the dead (i.e., a burial and resurrection).

There are individuals today who teach that an individual is saved merely by believing in Christ (i.e., by faith only). They will base this on John 3:16 and/or Acts 16:31. This is further reinforced with the use of what is commonly called "the sinner's prayer," a prayer that was developed by American evangelists from the late eighteenth century. Yet, throughout the book of Acts we do not see a person "believing and saying the sinner's prayer." We see something vastly different. Belief—or faith only—was "disconnected" from other essential elements of coming to salvation. It is obvious that people repented and turned to God (Acts 3:19). They openly and publicly confessed Christ. Moreover, they were immediately baptized. They did not postpone being baptized in order to take a three-month class preparing them spiritually to be baptized. Nor did they diminish the role of baptism in coming to Christ.

Over and again, people came to believe that Jesus was the Christ, the Son of the living God, and they were immediately baptized. This is consistently the pattern (See Acts 2:40-41—believers on the Day of Pentecost; 8:12—Philip in Samaria; 8:35-37—Philip and the Ethiopian; 9:17-18—the Apostle Paul's conversion; Acts 10:44-48—Cornelius and others; Acts 16:14-15—Lydia and her household; Acts 16:30-33—the Philippian jailer and his household; Acts 18:8—Paul in Corinth; Acts 19:1-5—Paul in Ephesus; Acts 22:16—Paul's testimony of his conversion). The New Testament Church clearly did not teach a "faith only" doctrine, but they practiced the importance of belief, repentance, confession and baptism in the salvation moment.

As well, the early Church taught that there was one baptism (see Ephesians 4:4-6), not multiple baptisms. When a person is baptized, the individual "puts on Christ," and is clothed in a "robe of righteousness" (see Galatians 3:26-27, Isaiah 61:10) that only Christ can provide. Our sins are forgiven—washed away in the moment of baptism by the blood of Christ (see Acts 2:38, 22:16)—not only in the past and the present, but also all future sins are forgiven because we are "clothed with Christ in baptism." There is no need to be repeatedly baptized with every sin we commit. Moreover, there is no second baptism in terms of a baptism of the Holy Spirit. When we believe, repent, confess and are baptized, we are baptized in the Holy Spirit in that we receive Him as a gift from God (see Acts 2:38), for there is "one baptism."

Finally, it is important to make a lifelong <u>commitment</u> to follow Christ. In Revelation 2:10b we are told to "be faithful to the point of death" and we will be given the crown of life. This phrase can be interpreted in two ways: we can be faithful until drawing our last breath in our old age, or we can be faithful to the point of being willing to die for our faith in Christ (i.e., being martyred).

 When we enter into a relationship with Jesus Christ, we become a part of the body of Christ—the Church (represented by the upper right circle). While in the Church, we grow in spiritual maturity (see 2 Peter 3:18). We minister to one another in the different seasons of life (see Romans 12:15). We worship/learn together, pray together, fellowship together, and remember the Lord's death together (see Acts 2:42). Being a part of the Church should be a life-changing experience in community.

Then, when we die, we are ushered into heaven (represented by the top circle) by the grace and mercy of God! Much like the Apostle Paul, we are then able to say, "I have fought the good fight, finished the race, kept the faith. Now there is in store for me a crown of righteousness, which the Lord, the righteous Judge, will award to me on that day, and not only to me, but to all who have longed for His appearing" (see 2 Timothy 4:7-8). We then spend all of eternity with the Lord in paradise.

Yet, there remains an unidentified "circle" (see bottom right). We could label this circle "apostasy." Apostasy is the rejection of one's beliefs. Just as a person has free will in accepting Christ, an individual has free will to reject Jesus Christ. This is a most serious state in which to be, and it is reached only after a person allows his or her heart to become hard and calloused towards God. There are verses in the Scriptures that make mention of apostasy (see Hebrews 3:12, 6:4-6, 10:26; I Timothy 4:1). Should a person die in this state (i.e., having rejected Jesus Christ as Savior), the individual will experience hell and the wrath of God for he or she no longer has Christ.

Looking at this chart, we clearly know that we are not in the "hereafter." Rather, we are in the "here-and-now." So, draw two horizontals lines directly under "heaven" and directly above "hell". Everything between those two lines represents the here and now, while everything outside of those lines represents the hereafter. Moreover, we can only be in one place at one time. So then, where are you? Where am I in this journey with Christ? Here's a challenge. Determine where "X" marks the spot. Place an "X" on the diagram representing where you currently see yourself spiritually. Is there a need to be moving on down the road" spiritually? Is it time to finally believe in Christ? Is it time to repent and turn from sin? Is it time to go public with a decision for Christ? Is it time to be baptized into Christ? "X" marks the spot.

☺**Reflection Question:** What is the biggest obstacle that prevents you from evangelizing? What are the internal obstacles (fear, shyness, guilt, ignorance, etc.)? What about external (work rules, position, pressure)? Describe them! What has to change about <u>you</u> to overcome any of these obstacles?

As elders, we must lead by example and that means we must make an effort at bringing lost people to Christ. In order to do just that, we must personally know people who are not yet in the faith. Think of it this way. Retired NFL receiver Jerry Rice was once asked why he attended Mississippi Valley State University, a small college in Itta Bena, Mississippi. Though the large universities, like UCLA, had courted Rice with letters and cards, only Mississippi Valley State made a personal visit to Rice at his home. MSVU showed a personal interest in Rice, and that's what enabled them to close the deal with him. In the same way, we must invest personally in the lives of those who are not yet in the faith. By doing so, we will earn the privilege of sharing the gospel with these individuals, speaking candidly into their lives because we take an authentic interest in them. This will require us to take an inventory of our friendships and honestly assess how many spiritually lost people we personally know. If you are like me, the numbers of non-believing friends in your life are few. It is essential that we risk getting acquainted and involved with others who are not in the faith—hoping to enjoy such friendships.

☺**Reflection Question:** Develop a strategy for reaching someone using the chart below:

Individual's Name?	
Relationship?	
Place and Time?	
How will you generically start	

the conversation? How will you introduce Christ into it?	
What are some possible obstacles to overcome?	
What if he/she says "no"?	
What is he/she says "yes"?	

Conclusion & Challenge

In *Kon-Tiki: Across the Pacific by Raft*, Thor Heyerdahl related how he and five others crossed the Pacific Ocean from South America to the South Pacific Islands on a raft of balsa logs tied together with hemp ropes. During their three month trek in 1947, the crew of six had little to no ability to steer the raft. Moreover, when something fell off the raft into the water, it was nearly impossible to recover the item as it was quickly carried away on the current.

Two months into the journey, while thousands of miles from land, one of the crew fell into the ocean. Strong wind and currents quickly put distance between the raft and Herman Watzinger, the man who went overboard. With time passing quickly and the distance of separation growing greater, Watzinger became nothing more than a dot on the seascape. Putting on a life belt tied to a belt, Knute Haugland dove into the waves, swam to Watzinger, grabbed him tightly, and the men on the raft pulled them back to the raft— saving their lives. Haugland risked his life to save a friend.

When was the last time you took a risk to bring the news of salvation to a friend? Do you recall that individual's name? Do you recall the day, time, and place when you baptized that individual into the death and resurrection of Jesus Christ? If elders are not leading others to Christ, we are failing to be the leaders God expects us to be. We must courageously take risks to reach those who are spiritually lost, for if we fail to take such risks, the distance between us will grow far too great. In the ocean, this growing distance is called the leeway effect. When floating in the water, ocean currents move an object in one direction, while wind currents move objects floating on top of the water in another. Could there be a relational leeway effect between we, who are saved, with those who are spiritually lost? As leaders of the church, we must intentionally risk closing this gap, making sure that distance does not keep us apart from those who need us most.

Endnotes

---

[1] Thom S. Rainer, "First-person: The Dying American Church," *SBC Baptist Press*, March 28, 2006, www.bpnews.net/bpcolumn.asp?ID= 2197.

Chapter 5

Enjoying...Your Fellow Elders

Gary L. Johnson

"Two are better than one because they have a good return for their work.
If one falls down, his friend can help him up.
But pity the man who falls and has no one to help him up!"
King Solomon, *Ecclesiastes* 4:9-10

On a visit to the Alamo in San Antonio, Texas, I had the opportunity to do research in the archives and discovered a most interesting fact about one of the Alamo freedom fighters. No known picture exists of James Butler Bonham, a hero of the Alamo. But in the archives, there is a picture of his nephew, Major James Bonham, who bore a striking resemblance to his uncle. The Bonham family donated the picture of the nephew so that people could know the appearance of the James Butler Bonham, the one who died for freedom. In much the same manner, there is no literal portrait of Jesus, the one who died for our freedom from sin, but His likeness is to be seen in His people.

Genesis 1:26 declares that we have been made in the image of God, meaning that we have the potential to reflect His divine nature and attributes. Moreover, Genesis 1:26 specifically states "Let us make man in our image..." The verse indicates the triune nature of God, existing as Father, Son and Spirit. God is in relationship, and we should be in relationship, as well.

While incarnate, Jesus had a relationship-rich life. Jesus had occasional contact with the most number of people (i.e., the multitudes), such as when He preached the Sermon on the Mount or multiplied the fish and the loaves. There was a large group of people who met with Jesus when He appeared to five hundred believers following His resurrection (see 1 Corinthians 15:6). He spent more time training and equipping seventy-two of His followers before sending them out two-by-two (see Luke 10:1, 17). Yet, Jesus spent the majority of His time with the twelve disciples. For a little over three years, Jesus invested His life in developing their lives. He was counting on these men to take His good news to others. Even out of these twelve, Jesus spent unique moments with the inner circle—James, Peter and John—when He took them to 1) the top of the mount of transfiguration, 2) to witness the healing of Jairus' daughter, and 3) to pray with Him in the Garden of Gethsemane the night prior to His death.

We are Relational

In much the same way, we are to be relational. We have occasional contact with "multitudes" in that we are a part of the community in which we live. We spend some amount of our time in worship with people in the congregation we serve. We may be in a part of a large group, such as a men's ministry team in the church that meets periodically. Yet, we must be a part of a small group of people. This could be an in-home Bible study for couples, a men's small group Bible study, etc. These are the individuals with whom we are spending the majority of our time in Christian community. Yet, like Jesus, we must have an inner circle of men with whom to do life, and it is in this inner circle that we experience the deepest of Christian brotherhood and accountability. A great place to find such friends is in the eldership. From among our fellow elders, we can develop deep friendship so that it can be said of us that we are a band of brothers (see Figure 5.1).

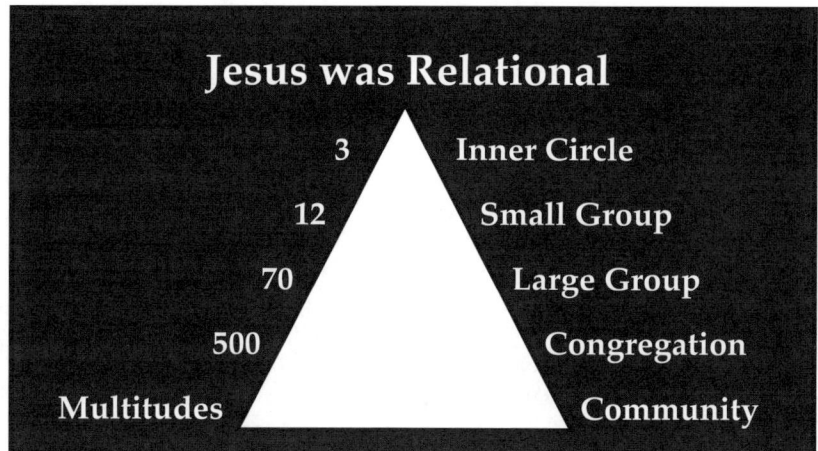

Figure 5.1

😊**Reflection Question:** Given the diagram above, where is your relational comfort level as an elder of the church? Can you name the men who are in your inner circle? If not, why not?

Regretfully, many of us do not enjoy our fellow elders as close friends. We have fallen victim to the phenomenon of being a friendless American male. Most men have a difficult time enjoying one another in authentic friendship. It seems that a mystery shrouds the concept of male friendship. When the western frontier was being forged in the 1800s, a rugged individualism enabled men to survive the life-threatening trek out west. Though the west has been won, could it be that we still live with a spirit of rugged individualism—believing that we do not need other men in our lives—which prevents us from experiencing deep brotherhood as men of God?

If it's not rugged individualism, maybe its rigid isolationism that keeps us apart from one another. Have you noticed how isolated we live our lives? Rugged individualism leads to rigid isolation. When we look closely at our culture, it appears that Americans are some of the loneliest people in the world. Other cultures celebrate deep community by moving towards one another in friendship.

We're moving away from one another in friendship. Think of it this way.

When I was a boy growing up, we lived in a neighborhood where the yards were small and the houses were close to one another, as well as being close to the street. A sidewalk stretched up and down the block in front of the houses, and houses had a front porch where people would sit in close proximity to the people walking on the sidewalk. A very common sight would be to notice different neighbors sitting on one another's porch visiting with one another. Our family knew every family living in every house on both sides of our street for the entire block. We even had a summer block party where we had games for the neighborhood children while meat was being grilled and food was being served. When a neighbor died, someone went door to door to collect money to buy flowers from the neighborhood and to arrange meals for the grieving family. Houses also had screen doors to keep the summer bugs out, while letting the cool air inside. Yet, a screen door did something more—it served as a warm welcome to people standing just outside. A screen door was not a barrier to keep people out so much as it was a simple way to let people inside of your home.

So much has changed in this one generation. We have screens today, but they look and serve in much different ways. Modern-day screens are caller ID, enabling us to screen our phone calls, choosing which ones we take while we push the others to voice mail. Instead of enjoying conversation with one another, friends now depend on texting and e-mail as primary conduits of communication. Technology enables us to move away from people and not towards them. ATMs enable us to do our banking without having to talk with a teller. We can pay for fuel at the pump so that we don't have to speak with a clerk. We can do a great deal of our shopping over the internet so that we don't have to leave the house—avoiding all manner of contact with people. Some people have moved out into the country so that homes are situated on spacious areas of land and not in neighborhoods with small yards. Some homes have been built far from the sidewalk, having exchanged a front porch for a back deck that is surrounded by a tall privacy fence. So much has changed in one generation, and frankly, our friendships have suffered as a result. People are deliberately moving away from one another, not towards one another, in friendship. If we avoid people at all cost, it will cost us in the end.

☺**Reflection Question:** On the scale provided below, where do you tend to reside relationally? Do you tend toward isolationism or individualism? Why do you say this about yourself? Explain.

Isolationism◄─────────┼─────────┼─────────┼──────►Individualism

Removing Relational Barriers

As men of God, we must move in each other's direction to enjoy Christian brotherhood. For that to happen, we must remove barriers that tend to keep us apart from one another. It is very common for us to build relational barriers in our lives and not to recognize those barriers between us. The following are five barriers that I must continually work to overcome if I am to enjoy an inner circle of Christian brotherhood with my closest of friends.

Barrier #1: My Inclination to be Competitive

Men want to win at all costs. We hate to lose at anything. Coach Vince Lombardi was often heard saying, "Winning isn't everything, it's the only thing!" Speaking for myself, I am highly competitive in nature. If I am playing a particular sport, I want to win—or be on the winning team. Yet, the same is true in my work as a minister, in my home life as a husband-dad-grandfather, etc. I want to "win", leading a healthy church and enjoying a healthy family. I must confess that there are far too many times when I compare my life to others in the context of being competitive and wanting to come out on top. This attitude serves as a barrier, keeping me from enjoying authentic friendship with other Christian brothers.

Barrier #2: My Inability to Ask for Help

Pride keeps me from asking someone for help, and not only me, but many other men struggle with this barrier. Having been taught from an early age to not depend on anyone, we tend to be very independent in nature. When we cannot admit that we need help, we've then built a barrier between us.

Barrier #3: My Inhibitions to Enjoy Guy Company

Why is it that we need to have some sort of an agenda to get together? If a guy asks me to have lunch with him, one of my first questions is, "What do you want to talk about?" My first question is not, "Where and when?" so much as, "Why? What's up?" Men typically must have a reason for getting together instead of simply being able to enjoy each other's company.

Barrier #4: My Inhibition to Show Emotions

I can't speak for you, but I'm not going to cry in front of you. I'm not going to let you know if I am frightened, anxious, worried, depressed, etc. More than anything, I want you to think that I've got my act together, so if you ask me how I'm doing, the answer will always be "fine," even though life may be far from fine.

Barrier #5: My Inadequate Role Models

Don't look to Hollywood for any good role models when it comes to male friendship. Men are not doing life in deep, abiding friendship on the silver screen. Moreover, we typically do not see our dads living this way. I was a BUICK: a brought up in church kid. We went to church Sunday after Sunday, but I never saw my dad have significant friendships with other men of faith. So much of life is "caught" rather than "taught". We learn by example. So when we did not see our fathers modeling what healthy Christian friendship looks like, we have no example to follow. This void then becomes a barrier to me—and to you. At some point in time we must break this cycle and provide for younger men and boys a strong example of what an inner circle of Christian brothers is to be like. We can only do that if we move toward one another in friendship, and not away from one another.

☺**Reflection Question:** Using the five barriers listed above, rank these relational barriers from the one most prevalent in your life (position 1) to the one least present in your life (position 5). Offer comment or explanation if you can.

Pos.	Barrier	Comment
①		
②		
③		
④		
⑤		

So, how do we actually do that? How do we move toward one another in Christian friendship? How do elders become close friends in the faith? Can we actually experience authentic brotherhood or is it far too difficult to pursue?

Think of it this way. Mensa is an organization whose members are incredibly intelligent, having a measurable IQ of 140 or greater. MSN reported that a Mensa convention was held in San Francisco, and a number of delegates decided to eat lunch together at a nearby restaurant. While sitting at the table, they discovered that their saltshaker contained pepper and the peppershaker was full of salt. They began discussing how to exchange the contents of the bottles without spilling any of the salt and pepper, and making the exchange by using only the implements that were on the table—that being a straw, a napkin and a saucer. They used their collective genius, developed a game-winning strategy, and then called their server to the table to impress her with their solution. When they pointed out to the server that the salt and pepper shakers contained the wrong contents, she did two things immediately: 1) she apologized to them for the inconvenience, and 2) she simply unscrewed the caps of each shaker and switched them to their rightful place![1] Moral of the story: we often make things more complicated and difficult than they are intended to be—like that of enjoying authentic Christian friendship with other men of faith. So, here are some simple, practical suggestions that I have found helpful to me in developing deeper friendships with my fellow elders.

Suggestion #1: Follow the Biblical Model

Have you noticed all of the famous pairs in the Bible? They stretch from cover to cover. We read of David and Jonathon, Elijah and Elisha, Moses and Joshua, Paul and Barnabas, Peter and John. Men of God were doing life together. It's important to note that Jesus trained His disciples and then sent them out "two by two" (see Mark 6:6-7). Why did He do that? He could have advanced His teaching in a much greater way had He sent them out individually. Why two by two? The answer is obvious. As a Jewish boy, Jesus learned the Old Testament while growing up, and an important lesson He would have heard was from Ecclesiastes 4:9-12, which states "two are better than one." Jesus was following the biblical model, and we must do the same.

As boys, we grew up watching the antics of "famous pairs" on the television; such as those of Lucy Ricardo and Ethyl Mertz, Wally Cleaver and Eddie Haskell, the Lone Ranger and Tonto, Sheriff Andy Taylor and his sidekick Barney Fife. Then along came Batman and Robin, Charlie Brown and Snoopy, Bert and Ernie, and we can't forget Beavis and the other guy. Friendship is ingrained in our American culture, but more importantly, it is taught in the Word of God. So, elders can and should move towards one another in authentic friendship by simply following the biblical model. Become a modern day "famous pair."

Suggestion #2: Center the Friendship on God

Some friendships become great friendships because of a common interest. For example, some guys develop an authentic friendship because they both enjoy hunting, fishing or a particular sport. I enjoy mountain climbing with some guys from the church, and over the years, we have formed a bond of friendship that is uncommonly strong. Yet, when it comes to friendship between the elders, there is a mutual interest that must bind us together, and that interest must be our walk with God. In 1 Samuel 18, Jonathon and David met one another for the first time. David had just conquered Goliath in hand-to-hand combat, and it's obvious from reading the text that Jonathon saw the whole thing. He saw David oppose the enemy. He heard David defy the enemy in the name of the Lord. Moreover, when Jonathon witnessed the courage of David, something stirred within him. It's no wonder that we read that "Jonathon became one in spirit with David" (1 Samuel 18:1). Both men had a passion for defending God's people by defeating God's enemies. These two men were on the same page spiritually. What mattered to God, mattered to them. God was at the center of their lives, and as a result, he was at the center of their friendship. This same phenomenon should be true in our brotherhood as elders.

Suggestion #3: Invest in the Friendship

Notice in 1 Samuel 18:3 that Jonathon made a covenant with David. Throughout their story, their friendship is described as a covenant (see 1 Samuel 20:8, 16-17, 42; 23:18).   The word "covenant" is from a Hebrew word with multiple meanings, one of which is "to chain, to fetter."   Jonathon and David chained themselves to one another in friendship. Notice verses 3-4 that Jonathon gave David his robe and tunic (i.e., military uniform), his sword, bow and belt, even though there were only two swords in all of Israel at the time (see 1 Samuel 13:16-22).   When Jonathon gave David his robe, he acknowledged by his actions that David would someday be king of Israel. Still, there came a time when Jonathon verbally declared that David would be king some day and that he would be second to the throne (see 1 Samuel 23:17).   David and Jonathon invested in their friendship, and it was an investment that paid off. After Jonathon was killed in battle (see 1 Samuel 31:2), David cared for his son, Mephibosheth, for years to come (see 2 Samuel 9:1-10). Do you and I have a friend—a brother in Christ—with whom we have made a covenant? Have we "chained ourselves" to a brother in Christ with whom to do life for years yet to come? Will we care for and look after his widow and family should he predecease us? We can make this kind of a covenant with a friend only if God is at the center of our friendship, and there is no better brother with whom to enjoy covenant friendship with than a fellow elder.

Suggestion #4: Be Helpful

When we read the story of Job, we often think of his three friends in a critical manner. Yet, what we need to do is give them credit for where credit is due. The three guys—Eliphaz, Bildad, and Zophar—all met by agreement to go and sympathize with Job. Think that through. They could not send a quick note of encouragement via e-mail. They couldn't pick up their cell phones and give Job a quick call to check on him. They went to him. If they were businessmen, they put up a "closed sign" for a number of days in order to be of help to their friend. In that era, they did not have PTO (paid time off) accruing on the job. They kissed their wives good-bye, hugged their kids, and then walked some distance to be with their friend in need. Granted, they blew it once they spent some time with him, criticizing him for an apparent moral lapse in his life, which resulted in uncommon suffering from the wrath of God. Their good intentions were lost because of some bad assumptions.

Like the three guys, we want to be quick to respond with help to a close brother in Christ, and we want to follow through with continuing help. I'm reminded of how devastated young John Mark had to have been when the Apostle Paul refused to let him continue with them on the mission trail (see Acts 15:36-39). Yet, Barnabas, the Son of Encouragement, took young John Mark under wing and traveled with him to Cyprus. Mark was a cousin of Barnabas (Colossians 4:10), and Cyprus was home to Barnabas (Acts 4:36). So, we have a picture of a strong man of God taking a wounded younger man of God back home. At home, they would have recuperated and healed. We can speculate that John Mark continued in ministry because a friend was exceptionally helpful to him. I wonder if we would have the Gospel of Mark today if it hadn't been for the helpful, healing nature of Barnabas towards young John Mark. Are we helpful to one another as fellow elders? Like Barnabas, do we draw alongside one another when we struggle in life? If elders are to be present in the broken lives of those in the local church, we should be able and willing to do the same with one another.

Suggestion #5: Speak the Truth

In Ephesians 4:15, Paul reminds us to speak the truth in love. In order for our friendships to be deep and rewarding, we must go deeper in conversation with one another. This is a real challenge, not only for men, but for Americans. If we are to have authentic, deep friendship with a brother in Christ, there must be deep, honest conversation that is spoken in love. We are challenged in Proverbs 27:17 to sharpen one another, even as iron sharpens iron when struck together. That phenomenon can only happen with deeper conversation. Likewise, Proverbs 27:6 states that "faithful are the wounds of a friend", meaning when we speak truth to one another, do not speak it in such a way as to hurt one another, deliberately wounding a brother. No, speak the truth in love, wanting to sincerely help a brother become a stronger man of God for the glory of God. When we do so, we are investing in a friendship that is centered on God.

☺**Reflection Question:** How can you implement these suggestions in your own life? What about in the life of the eldership as a whole? How does the eldership compare to these suggestions at present? How can you improve their relationship?

Reporting to One Another

One last issue we have to deal with when it comes to our friendship with fellow elders is that of being accountable. As men of God, we must hold one another accountable in our Christian walk. It's pretty easy to spot accountability on the pages of Scripture. For example, in Job 1:6-7, Satan appeared before God, and God held him accountable with the question, "Where have you come from?" In other words, "What have you been up to, Satan? Report in!" In Mark 6:7, Jesus sent the disciples out two-by-two, and when they returned, they "reported in" to Jesus (see Mark 6:30), sharing with Him all that they had done while away. Even Paul and Barnabas were held accountable by the elders of the Church in Jerusalem. Once they arrived in Jerusalem, they appeared before the apostles and elders as they "reported everything God had done through them" while on the mission field in Antioch (Acts 15:4).

What makes us think that we don't need to "report in" with one another? The writer of Hebrews declared, "Obey your leaders and submit to their authority. They keep watch over you as men who must give an account" (13:17). If there is to be a submissive, obedient spirit of accountability of believers to elders, should not the same submissive, obedient spirit of accountability exist between us as elders? Shouldn't we want to be accountable to one another? God has blessed me with a close brother. Like me, he serves as a preacher and an elder of a nearby church. We talk together and even get together a few times each week. We've known one another for years, and we have invested in each other's life, making certain that God is at the center of our friendship. We often find ourselves talking with one another at very deep levels, being honest and painfully candid. These candid conversations happen when we hold one another accountable as men of God. Any number of questions can be used in holding one another accountable, but the following is our list. We often make the time to ask these questions of one another (*which should be used as a reflection exercise both individually/privately, but then done corporately with one another*).

- How's your soul? Be specific.
- How have you spent time with Jesus?
- In what ways are you loving your wife as Christ loves His Church?
- Are you seeking her best? How?
- Have you fought with her this week? Why?
- Are you emotionally tempted?
- How are you disciplining your eyes sexually?
- Have you been alone with a woman not your wife?
- Have you spent time with your children? Doing what?
- Who's responsible for your success: yourself or God?

- Is your pride out of whack?
- Did you just lie to me in responding to any of these questions?

Conclusion

AOL News reported an incredible story. Two guys worked together every day for a furniture delivery company. Gary would lift one end of the couch while Randy would lift the other end. People often told them that they looked alike, but they said it was just coincidence. Randy had been researching his family history. He found out that he was adopted, and a new law in the state of Maine allowed him to see his birth certificate. While doing some research, he learned that both his parents had died, but that they had another son, born June 10, 1974. While on a furniture delivery run, the two guys heard those ever-familiar words, calling attention to the fact that they resembled one another. Now knowing that he had a brother, Randy decided to ask Gary some personal questions—like when his birthday is. When Gary told Randy his birth date, he realized why they resembled one another – they were biological brothers! They had grown up in neighboring towns, attended rival schools, and were only one year apart in age. Their story appeared in the local paper, and they were further startled when a woman contacted them after she read their story and realized they were her half-brothers. She showed up at their workplace with her birth certificate, showing her new-found brothers that that their mother gave birth to her a few years earlier.[2] For the first time in their lives, they came to realize that they were family to one another.

Think that through with me. Two guys working side by side, day after day, and they didn't even realize they were family. Could that resemble us? As brothers, we serve side by side, year after year, as elders of the local church. Yet, are we living in such a way that we don't even know that we are family? When will we realize that we are brothers—bound to one another by the most priceless blood—that being the blood of Christ? I can't imagine life without friends, particularly those friends who serve alongside me as fellow elders of Christ.

Endnotes

[1]http://www.preachingtoday.com/illustrations/article_print.html?id=24786

[2] AOL News (9-19-09), quoting an article entitled "Adopted brothers reunited by work," from the Bangor Daily News and The Nashua Telegraph (9-22-09)

Chapter 6

Enjoying Difficult People

David Roadcup

"If it is possible, as far as it depends on you, live at peace with everyone." Romans 12:18

"Irritation in the heart of a believer is always an invitation to the devil to stand by." Eleanor Doan

Strange title for a book chapter, isn't it? "Enjoying Difficult People?" Why not "Enduring Difficult People", "Erasing Difficult People" or "Eliminating Difficult People"? Why "Enjoying Difficult People"?

Difficult people are part of most aspects of life and most church families. They are a reality. This will never change. As long as humanity is on the earth, there will be people who call on, try and test our emotional, spiritual and mental reserves. It is true in our personal lives, our family relationships, at work and in the church. It is simply a fact of life. Church leaders are painfully aware of this reality. Lyle Schaller writes, "Nearly every congregation includes a couple of members the leaders wish had joined the church across the street or down the road. These are the people nearly every member finds it difficult to get along with in a satisfying manner. Some pastors insist the church tends to attract, in disproportionately large numbers, the neurotic, the lonely, the hostile, and the maladjusted personalities."[1]

This insight calls for this chapter to be included in a book on effective elder relationships. Although difficult people are challenging and stressful to deal with at times, their presence and participation in the life of a congregation can be a blessing in disguise.

Charles Keating tells us, "Difficulty can be a value. It is not always negative. Difficulty can be perceived as enrichment, an added motivation and source of cohesion; if it is, then difficult people can be a source of enriching stimulation and deepening relationships."[2] They can stretch us in several ways:

- *Difficult people can teach us about grace.* Each one of us requires a measure of the Lord's grace. As we experience that grace in our walk, we are grateful. In the same manner, those in the church family who are difficult, obstinate and abrasive need grace for their actions. In leadership circles, these folks are referred to as "EGRs" (Extra Grace Required). As we receive grace, we should be giving grace. Remember, every believer, difficult ones included, is important to God. God is concerned with growing healthy believers as well as those who struggle. As we grant grace, we will receive grace and grow through its presence in our lives as leaders. The reflection of grace as it is extended to those who need it should remind those us of our need for grace, as well.

- *Difficult people test our maturity as leaders.* When it comes to we who lead the church, wisdom and discernment should be a significant part of our leadership. This is especially true when it comes to our flock. Our first and foremost responsibility is to shepherd, nurture, encourage and protect our people. We take care of those who are pleasant and healthy as well as those who are struggling.

  - *Difficult people provide opportunities for self-examination.* When a difficult person presents a problem, it gives us an opportunity to ask ourselves, "Does this person have a legitimate point?" "Is this something I/we should look at?"

Mark Rosen tells us, "Your antagonist is indeed a teacher, an unwitting envoy of a universe that wants you to grow."[3] And again, "Difficult people are teachers who help us to develop in a fashion that can only take place when we are forced to face and surmount an unwelcome challenge. Difficult people impel us to rise to the occasion.[4] A friend of mine who is a professional Christian counselor tells me that "even in the harshest of unfair criticism, there is often 1% - 2% of truth that should be examined and pondered."[5]

How we react to difficult people and their behavior is a test of our implementation of Scriptural relational principles. Scripture tells us how to respond when difficult situations present themselves. Effective leaders follow the teachings of patience, forbearance, self-control, careful thought and action. When called upon to deal with a difficult person, our patience and forbearance will be strengthened as we do the right thing in dealing with those who need help. Dealing with difficult people is always a stretching experience.

Let us not, then, always see difficult people as an obstacle or problem. We can find ways to be thankful for their presence and participation in the life of our church.

☺Reflection Question: Can you think of an instance wherein a difficult person(s) produced any of these "positive" effects on you? What did you learn from the encounter(s)? How did it make you a better elder?

Describing Difficult People

Supportive members of the congregation have the right to ask for information about issues, policies and financial matters in the life of the church. People are not classified as difficult because they ask questions to seek clarification. There needs to be a balance in which the elders and staff hold the congregation accountable. The other side of the continuum is the congregation holding the elders and staff accountable. This balance indicates a healthy congregational life. When one of these aspects of the church is not functioning, there can be serious trouble.

Difficult people are in a different category.

Who are difficult people? They are people who are normally unhappy, frustrated, individuals. They desire to have control and enjoy being on top. They may suffer from depression. They may be fearful. They may have severe insecurity issues. They do not lack for numerous opinions on various topics. Some have the tendency to beef, bite and bellyache about issues and decisions in church life. Some gossip. Many maintain a critical, negative and divisive spirit. Difficult people may not know they are out of step with the rest of the congregation. Some are angry and communicate that fact. They may feel entitled. They may be envious. They can be combative, even abusive. Inflexibility is many times part of their makeup. Difficult people, in most cases, are spiritually blind. They may have medical or psychiatric issues. They may also be affected by the demonic.

When a difficult person surfaces in a congregation, conflict, strife and struggle can emerge. This type of behavior disrupts, damages and can eventually devastate a church, if not carefully handled by the leadership team. Elders should know that one really negative, critical person or family who is allowed to spread their influence in a church can bring an entire church to its knees in terms of its mission and forward momentum.

In many cases, difficult people have suffered deep wounds in their past. When the process of "working through" and the work of forgiveness does not occur, the result of these wounds begins to affect the life and relationships of the person who was wounded. Many times, anger, bitterness, rage and the perceived loss of control plague the person. Remember, *hurting people hurt people.*

Unresolved hurt and the resultant anger can express itself in what is known as "transference". Transference is defined as "the shift of emotions, especially those experienced in childhood, from one person or object to another, especially the transfer of feelings about a parent to an analyst.[6] The concept of "kicking the cat" is a great example of transference. A man's boss shouts at him at work and he goes home and "kicks the cat" or yells at his wife or children. In many instances, people who have been hurt and not done the work of forgiveness will bring those hurts to church with them. Sometimes difficult people see members of their church family as safe people to receive their barbs because, in most cases, church people are not quick to "give it back" or retaliate.

Difficult people have a penchant for creating conflict. Conflict is defined as, "a direct disagreement of ideas or interests, a battle or struggle, antagonism or opposition." [7] Kenneth Haugk describes the person who is an antagonist by writing, "Antagonists are individuals who, on the basis of *non-substantive evidence, go out of their way* to make *insatiable demands*, usually attacking the person or performance of others. These attacks are *selfish in nature, tearing down rather than building up*, and are frequently directed against those in a leadership capacity."[8] Robert Dale states, "I'm thinking of the congregational mismatch, the square peg in the round hole. These folks have a barb, a rough spot, an abrasive characteristic. They probably rub many other persons the wrong way. Like oil and water, they don't mix or fit in well with the majority of the congregation. They are out-of-step in some way or out-of-sync on some issue. While 'fit' is a two-way street, the difficult church member is a misfit within his congregation in some obvious way."[9]

☺**Reflection Question:** Reflecting on the previous paragraphs, what kind of difficult people have you encountered? How did the list above help "tag" them? How did you deal with them? Was it effective or ineffective? Explain or illustrate.

The Behaviors of Difficult People

Difficult people exhibit behaviors that express their struggles and needs. The following word pictures describe different types of behavior that can be exhibited on the part of difficult people:

- *The Critic* – the person who constantly complains and gives unwanted advice.
- *The Martyr* - the person who is the victim and wracked with self-pity.
- *The Wet Blanket* – the person who is pessimistic and automatically negative.
- *The Steamroller* – the person who absolutely must have his or her own way.
- *The Gossip* – the person who spreads rumors and leaks secrets.
- *The Control Freak* – the person who is unable to let go and let be.
- *The Sniper* – the person who "shoots" from cover and cannot confront.
- *The Sherman Tank* – the person who bullies others.
- *The Volcano* – the person who explodes to gain control.
- *The Sponge* – the person who is constantly in need but never returns anything.
- *The Betrayer* – the person who is feigns loyalty but can betray acquaintances.

From where does the negative behavior exhibited by a difficult person come? Difficult people normally have major character flaws which explain much of their behavior. In his excellent book, *Handling*

Difficult People, John Townsend makes this point: "Behavior is a symptom of how a difficult person looks at life. Don't get sidetracked by behavior. The first thing to understand is a difficult person's *character*."[10]   Henry Cloud and John Townsend have defined character as "that set of abilities a person needs to meet the demands of life."[11] They propose that there are six basic aspects to character. They are the abilities to:

- Sustain meaningful relationships
- Take responsibility and have self-control in your life
- Live in the reality of your and others' imperfections
- Work and do tasks competently
- Have an internal moral structure
- Have a transcendent spiritual life[12]

When these abilities are present in a person's life, things usually go well. In the life of a difficult person, some or most of these abilities may be areas of struggle. Difficult people usually do not admit to the fact that their behavior is disruptive or hurting the church. They will maintain that they have the right to do what they want because their opinions and ideas are more important than those of others.

Church leaders should be aware of the warning signs which accompany difficult people and their behavior. Here are key examples:
- *A change or cooling in the relationship* – when a normally warm relationship begins to turn cool with no explanation, be aware. In many instances, the children or family members of difficult people will reflect what they have been hearing at home, as well. Difficult people will use relational signals to indicate that there may be an attack in the works.

- *"Concerns" expressed in a cloaked veneer of caring* – one author called these "honeyed concerns"[13] When a difficult person presents their concerns, they may come in the form of a visit or letter. Be aware that this may be the beginning of a situation that needs to be handled with wisdom and immediacy.
- *Criticism or "stirring of the pot"* – Staff, elders and other significant leaders may be in the "crosshairs" of difficult people. They may also criticize ministries, programming, new policies or change of some kind. These areas and people may be "lightening rods for difficult people.
- *The ceasing of financial contributions* – One of the ways difficult people will communicate their dissatisfaction is through the stopping of their financial participation. This move is characteristic of the childish behavior of the difficult person.
- *Collecting supporters* – Difficult people will "wave their flag" and at times, attempt to gain support from others in the church fellowship. When left unchecked, the grouping of people who "support the cause" may begin. This can begin by whispering in the hallway, by telephone, email or other social media. If and when this begins, the leadership must take wise action to protect the unity of the church.
- *Clandestine meetings* – Meetings may be organized that do not include any staff members or elders. These meetings are usually the hotbeds for serious and divisive discussions and actions.
- *Attacks or hurtful or negative opinions in public meetings* - Difficult people will use Sunday School classes, Adult Bible Fellowships, small home bible study and prayer groups, men's or women's groups or congregational meetings to express themselves publicly. This level of expression is extremely damaging. Intervention must be used to prohibit this from happening or continuing.

Reflection Question: Given these signs, think of the most recent "difficult person" you encountered in the church (shouldn't be hard). How many of these indicators did they trigger? How did these actions make you feel as an elder?

Dealing with Difficult People

There are times in a relationship or in church life where leadership must move due to the negative behavior of a difficult person or persons. When it is time for confrontation, discerning leaders construct a prayer forged plan that will produce the most beneficial outcome for the church and offending person(s) both, if possible. In initiating action, several considerations should be mentioned.

(1) In all things, we want to bring glory to God and work hard for His will to ultimately be done. Paul writes in 1 Corinthians 10: 31, "So whether you eat or drink or whatever you do, do it all for the glory of God."

(2) We want to protect the church and the ministry which God has established. Peter gives clear instructions when he states, "Be shepherds of God's flock that is under your care, serving as overseers…" (1 Peter 5:2)

(3) All things are to done carefully and in an orderly fashion (1 Cor. 14:40).

(4) When it comes to those involved in the offense, love and a desire for reconciliation should prevail. Paul states, "Make every effort to keep the unity of the Spirit through the bond of peace" (Eph. 4:3). Reconciliation and ministry to those who are offensive should be part of our goal as we seek to bring peace.

Working with Individuals and Groups

When a single individual is involved in conflict with the church, the best approach is simply to follow the guidelines which Jesus taught in Matt. 18:15-17. "If your brother sins against you, go and show him his fault, just between the two of you. If he listens to you, you have won your brother over. But if he will not listen, take one or two others along, so that 'every matter may be established by the testimony of two or three witnesses.' If he refuses to listen to them, tell it to the church; and if he refuses to listen even to the church, treat him as you would a pagan or tax collector." Jesus instructs us to go one-on-one to the person and talk to them about the offense. With a single difficult person, why not select someone from the leadership team or someone the leadership team has confidence in and ask them to approach the person in love and humility? Over breakfast, lunch or coffee, talk to the person and work to discover a resolution to whatever the problem might be.

When there is a problem with a married couple or family, why not have two members of the leadership team make an appointment to stop by their home and search for common ground and a solution to the problem at hand.

When there is a group of people who are dissatisfied, there are different approaches. First, the group can be divided up and approached individually (or by couple) and a resolution can be sought. If this is not possible, invite the group to meet with the ministers who might be directly involved and the elders, following the guidelines given below. The very worst way to handle a group of people who are causing difficulties is to call a congregational meeting and allow the disgruntled group to air their grievances in public before those who would attend the meeting. There is strength in numbers. This arrangement can (and usually does) end in serious damage to personal relationships and to the church, in general.

Steps to Reconciliation

When negative behavior on the part of offenders brings situations to the forefront, church leaders need to act. Whether it is gossip, sowing seeds of discord, creating disunity or organizing an attempt to divide the church, strong leaders initiate the following plan or one similar to bring about a solution to the problem.

Step 1 – Deciding When It Is Time To Act – When church elders and/or staff see a problem presenting itself, they must decide to act and to bring about a resolution to the problem. When people are being treated in an unchristian manner, when the unity of the church is being threatened or when serious offenses are being perpetrated, *leaders must act.*

An older attitude towards the behavior of difficult people was to simply ignore the problem their behavior was creating, hoping it would go away. When trouble spots occur, *ignoring them* is the worst thing the leadership team can do. Troubled situations normally get worse they are not confronted and carefully handled.

Step 2 – Collecting and Clarifying the Facts – Clear and accurate facts must be collected and understood before any formal action is taken. Operating on hear-say or rumor can get the process in serious trouble. Carefully document and obtain accurate information on all points of the offense.

Step 3 – Immerse the situation and all principals in prayer – Serious prayer is the greatest key to successfully completing a confrontation with an erring brother or sister or group of people. Ask the Lord to go before and prepare the hearts of everyone involved. Ask Him to bless the encounter, discussion and provide a positive outcome as a result of the meeting.

Step 4 – Self-examination - All leaders should examine their hearts in terms of motives and honesty about the situation at hand. Leaders should be careful to look into their hearts to make sure their motives and desires are pure as they approach the situation. Do we truly want the best outcome for everyone involved? Are we willing to lay aside any hurt or anger which has come to us over the offense as we begin the process of reconciliation?

Step 5 – Prepare a plan for a face-to-face meeting with those causing the offense – In order to hopefully bring about a peaceful outcome to the offensive situation, those leaders who are involved need to construct a plan for the meeting.   Below are important issues to consider:

a. Decide who will approach the offender(s). Two elders or an elder and staff member could be identified as those who will conduct the meeting. It goes without saying that a leader should never go by himself to conduct a confrontational meeting with multiple people present.

b. Record on paper exactly what the offense has been and what problems were created as a result of the difficult person's behavior for clarification purposes.

c. Contact the person(s) who will be requested to be at the meeting. Agree on meeting times and the place where the meeting will happen. The time of day of the meeting can be important. Later on in the evening, people usually have less of an energy level and less patience than in the morning hours. The place of the meeting is also import to consider. There are several possibilities.

- The church building. Reserving a room suitable for privacy and confidentiality would work. A room other than the minister's office is preferable.

- The offender's home. This would work as meeting in the home of the offender might possibly allow them to be more relaxed and make the confrontation proceed more smoothly. (Note – children and pets can be an issue if the meeting takes place in a home.)

- Restaurant or other public meeting place. This could be considered but the issue of confidentiality and having the ability to talk frankly in an uninterrupted manner might be marginalized.

d. Discuss how the offense will be presented to the offending party(s). Think through the wording and language that will be used to present the issue(s). Ken Sande, author of the excellent book titled *The Peacemaker* tell us, "Words play a key role in almost every conflict. When used properly, words promote understanding and encourage agreement. When misused, they usually aggravate offenses and drive people further apart."[14] It is important and necessary to discuss and go over how the main part of the conversation will be expressed. Also, remember that offering words of encouragement and support before the presentation of the offending issues will help the situation go more smoothly.

e. Meet with the principals at the appointed time and place. After social interaction has ended, express appreciation to those in attendance for their presence. Proceed to the discussion at hand. Plainly and clearly describe the problem(s) and issues that have arisen. Also discuss how the negative behavior/attitudes of those asked to the meeting have damaged the church and her forward movement.

f. Plan to ask the offenders for a response to the issue(s) being presented. Invite them to express themselves. Give them time to respond and explain their position.

g. Prepare for all levels of response. When entering into a meeting for confrontational purposes, it is a good idea to personally prepare for whatever may come as a result of the confrontation. To the positive, after being confronted, the offender may consider their actions, repent, ask forgiveness and express the desire for reconciliation. The other end of the spectrum would be the expression of extreme anger, shouting, name calling and explosive behavior. Prepare yourself for any or all of those reactions and all levels and responses in between. Think the situation through and discuss it together before the meeting. It is especially important for those leading to guard their responses and decide what they will do under all circumstances. *Prepare for anything.* "Often the greatest damage done is not done by the dragons themselves but by the overreactions they provoke in others. When attacked by dragons, our normal response is to become upset or defensive, and when we feel threatened, we usually windup dousing the fire with gasoline."[15]

h. Plan to hopefully arrive at an acceptable solution. The ideal would be to see a positive reconciliation through loving attitudes, patience and forbearance. If this does not happen, leaders must remain firm and decide on next steps.

In many instances, if conversation, even though it may be heated at times, continues, there can be a chance to reach an acceptable solution. If conversation ends abruptly or the meeting continues for a long period of time with no solution, the meeting may have to end without a clear resolution.

☺**Reflection Question:** Think of you last conflict situation. Which of the previous preparations would have been most helpful? What did you learn from experience and this chapter to be better prepared to deal with conflict?

Outcomes of Confrontations

Positive Outcomes – It is always the desire of leadership to see misbehavior or problems resolved in a loving and understanding way. This is the best of all endings to confrontation. We seek this outcome that the church may proceed and fulfill her mission.

Negative Outcomes – What happens if there is no clear, solid resolution? The leadership team prayed, planned and worked hard but the result was anger and bitterness on the part of the difficult person. "They didn't hear me" or "I was misunderstood!" are the responses of the offender.

Marshall Shelley in his excellent work, *Well Intentioned Dragons* states, "Despite our best efforts, the problems of contentious people are not quickly solved. Tensions can linger in limbo, no resolution in sight. Persistent resistance, nay-saying, and second-guessing seem to be the twentieth-century Western world's equivalent to persecution-a continuing threat to the health and growth of the church. Pastors dealing with dragons must learn to deal with unresolved situations – some temporarily until the dragon is tamed, appeased, or driven off..."[16]

The following are ways of handling a negative outcome:

(1) Maintain an open spirit - Continue to reach out to those creating the offense. Let them know that the leadership is willing to work together for a positive resolution.

(2) On-going prayer – Ask the Lord to move in the hearts and consciences of the offenders. The Holy Spirit is working in their lives. Pray for the Lord's will to be accomplished in the resolution of the situation.

(3) Give it time – Sometimes time can bring healing and soften difficult people. People should always be given the opportunity to heal and grow. Grant this grace with kindness and patience.

(4) Put them out – There are situations when prayer, time and discussion will not change the heart or attitude of a contentious or divisive person. When facing this situation, Scripture teaches us how to respond. We are to remove

them from the fellowship of the church. Paul tells, us, "Warn a divisive person once, and then warn him a second time. After that, have nothing to do with him. You may be sure that such a man is warped and sinful; he is self-condemned" (Titus 3:10-11).

☺**Reflection Question:** In your last encounter with a difficult church member, how did it end? Was it a positive or negative experience? What did you learn from it? What will you always do? Never do again?

A Final Word to Leaders

As we conclude, I want to encourage church leaders to keep in mind the balance between guarding the flock and managing the difficult issues in the life of the church and working with those who might have serious relational, spiritual and/or personal problems. Many times, people who struggle come to the church for help. In that process, they may cause problems and stress for the church and her leaders. While it is draining, stressful and time consuming, the Lord loves these people and we need to try to love them, as well. I would encourage all leaders to let agape love, patience, forbearance, wisdom and spiritual discernment guide them as they wisely deal with those who come under the category of "difficult people". "How would Jesus handle this person/situation?" is a good question to keep at the fore of all of our decisions. This is not to say that we do not take serious and firm action when it is needed. That can definitely be part of our ministry in dealing with difficult people. Maintaining the balance between grace and managing misbehavior in protecting the church is part of our ministry and calling. Let us do so with a spirit of love, maturity and wisdom and always a desire for reconciliation.

Endnotes

---

[1] Robert Dale, *Surviving Difficult Church Members* (Nashville, TN: Abingdon Press, 1984), 7.

[2] Charles Keating, *Dealing With Difficult People* (Ramsey, New Jersey: Paulist Press, 1984), 48.

[3] Mark I. Rosen, *Thank You for Being Such a Pain* (New York, New York: Harmony Books, 1998), 2.

[4] Ibid, 23.

[5] Gary Oliver in an interview, Highlands Ranch, CO, September 12, 1994

[6] Ereference from Dictionary.com

[7] Roy Lilley, *Dealing With Difficult People* (Philadelphia, PA: Replika Press, 2010), 24.

[8] Kenneth Haugk, *Antagonists in the Church* (Minneapolis, MN: Augsburg Publishing House, 1988), 25-26.

[9] Robert Dale, *Surviving Difficult Church Members* (Nashville, TN: Abingdon Press, 1984), 15.

[10] John Townsend, Handling Difficult People (Nashville, Tennessee: Thomas Nelson, 2006), 20.

[11] Ibid, 20.

[12] Ibid, 21.

[13] Kenneth Haugk, *Antagonists in the Church* (Minneapolis, MN: Augsburg Publishing House, 1988), 81.

[14] Ken Sande, *The Peacemaker* (Grand Rapids, MI, 2001), 146.

[15] Marshall Shelley, *Well-Intentioned Dragons* (Minneapolis, MN: Bethany House, 1994), 120-121.

[16] Ibid, 135.